# THE AMERICAN FLY FISHING EXPERIENCE

Theodore Gordon: His Lost Flies and Last Sentiments

*Theodore Gordon, Savannah, 1890*

**John Gubbins**

# THE AMERICAN FLY FISHING EXPERIENCE

## Theodore Gordon: His Lost Flies and Last Sentiments

Copyright © 2019 by John Gubbins. All rights reserved.

All Rights Reserved. No part of this book may be used or reproduced in any form or by electronic or mechanical means including photocopying, recording, or by any information storage and retrieval systems, without the expressed written permission of the author except by a reviewer who may quote brief passages in a review.

Published by: Brule River Press

Address all inquiries to:

John Gubbins

665 Tony's Lane, Ishpeming MI 49849

906-869-6679 • profoundriver@gmail.com

ISBN: 978-1-7334769-0-4

Library of Congress Control Number:

Cover Design: Nora Gubbins

Illustrated by: Nora Gubbins

Interior Layout: Stacey Willey, Globe Printing, Ishpeming MI

Author Photo Credit: Nora Gubbins

Every attempt has been made to source properly all quotes.

Printed in the United States of America

# Bert Darrow's Endorsement

Like many fly anglers and conservationists, I have tried to read as much written material as I could find about Theodore Gordon, whom we regard as the "Father of Dry Fly Fishing in America". John Gubbins, the author of "The American Fly Fishing Experience: Theodore Gordon: His Lost Flies and Last Sentiments", has given us insight into Gordon's life through both researching and reading written articles about him, doing important interviews of many knowledgeable people of Gordon and following in his footsteps to places where he lived and fished. With these facts and some fiction woven together, John Gubbins has given us a great insight into Gordon's life, as an angler, a fly tier, a writer, a person of many secrets and most importantly to me, a conservationist. I found it hard to put this book down once I started reading it. I highly recommend it as a must read to all anglers and conservationists.

~ *Bert Darrow,* President of the Theodore Gordon Flyfishers, Inc., Past President of the Catskill Fly Fishing Center and Museum, Permanent Director and Past President of the Catskill Mountains Trout Unlimited, protector of cold water fisheries, environmental activist, well traveled angler, licensed guide, and author of *Bert Darrow's Practical Fly Fishing: How to Cast and Fish Naturally* and the instructional video, *Tying Streamers and Bucktails in the Catskill Tradition.*

## Contents

McSherry's Saloon . . . . . . . . . . . . . . . . . . . . . 1

Dinner with Mrs. Henderson. . . . . . . . . . . . . . . 8

Jeanie Knight's Secret . . . . . . . . . . . . . . . . . . 20

Fly Tying. . . . . . . . . . . . . . . . . . . . . . . . . . . 24

Dinner with Mr. and Mrs. Henderson . . . . . . . . . 36

Savannah and the Habershams. . . . . . . . . . . . 46

Bread Board. . . . . . . . . . . . . . . . . . . . . . . . 57

My Color Spectrum . . . . . . . . . . . . . . . . . . . 60

Ham Sandwiches with Neyle . . . . . . . . . . . . . 70

My Uncle's Wall Street Office . . . . . . . . . . . . . 78

Favorite Flies . . . . . . . . . . . . . . . . . . . . . . . 89

Meeting Gail. . . . . . . . . . . . . . . . . . . . . . .105

The Bark Peelers' Stable. . . . . . . . . . . . . . . .111

Best Day, Best Year. . . . . . . . . . . . . . . . . . .115

Interview with Gail's Father . . . . . . . . . . . . . . . . .124

Parting. . . . . . . . . . . . . . . . . . . . . . . . . . . . . .133

Trophy Brown Trout . . . . . . . . . . . . . . . . . . . . .143

Jeanie's Treachery . . . . . . . . . . . . . . . . . . . . . . .147

Dinner with La Branche and Hewitt . . . . . . . . . .149

Plans for Writing a Book. . . . . . . . . . . . . . . . . .158

Dinner with Mrs. Henderson. . . . . . . . . . . . . . .162

Coma. . . . . . . . . . . . . . . . . . . . . . . . . . . . . . .173

Opening Day . . . . . . . . . . . . . . . . . . . . . . . . .179

My Nephew's Visit . . . . . . . . . . . . . . . . . . . . .187

Death . . . . . . . . . . . . . . . . . . . . . . . . . . . . . .193

Author's Afterword . . . . . . . . . . . . . . . . . . . . 209

BIBLIOGRAPHY . . . . . . . . . . . . . . . . . . . . . . .212

# Illustrations

FRONTISPIECE Theodore Gordon . . . . . . . . . . . . . i

ONE Gold Ribbed Hare's Ear. . . . . . . . . . . . . . . 25

TWO Quill Gordon . . . . . . . . . . . . . . . . . . . 34

THREE Beaverkill Run . . . . . . . . . . . . . . . . . 65

FOUR The Willowemoc Pool . . . . . . . . . . . . . . 66

FIVE The Beaverkill Embankment Pool . . . . . . . . . 67

SIX The Esopus Curving Run . . . . . . . . . . . . . . 68

SEVEN Cahill . . . . . . . . . . . . . . . . . . . . . . 92

EIGHT The Beaverkill Rapids . . . . . . . . . . . . . 117

NINE The Beaverkill Rock Face Pool . . . . . . . . . . 119

# Acknowledgments

With Special Gratitude:

To my wife Carol, a more patient person, a better angler, a better observer, and a more caring person than me.

To my fishing buddies, my son Alex and his wife Emily, my sister Nora, and my brother-in-law, James Roderick,

To our friends Beverley Matherne, Theo McCracken, Steve Pence, Teresa Frankovich, Keith Kendall, Chet DeFonso and Ron Hill.

To MD, manager of the Roscoe IGA Country Store, and to the wait staff of the Roscoe Diner.

## Author's Forward

If the celebrated fly fisher, Theodore Gordon, is to be believed, most of what you will read in this book is true. The stories recounted here Gordon told and retold about himself. Taken together, they add up to a kind of autobiography, for they portray Gordon as he saw himself. Gordon's stories involve his struggles with tuberculosis, his disastrous financial investments, his love and loss of a mysterious, young woman, his care for his mother, his life in Savannah, his days working on Wall Street, his Catskill friends, and his fishing experiences. Of special interest to the fly fisher are Gordon's stories of how he tied flies, the fly patterns he trusted, and his novel theory of "ringing the colors."

Gordon never considered himself the legend we have made of him. Although overbearing on occasion, he saw himself close to the bone. Once he summed up the import of his life as proving that British fly fishing methods do not work in America. This humble reading of his own significance freed him to embrace fully his American fly fishing experiences. While his contemporaries remained wedded to British flies and British methods, Gordon made his own way and so became the most inventive fly fisher of his age.

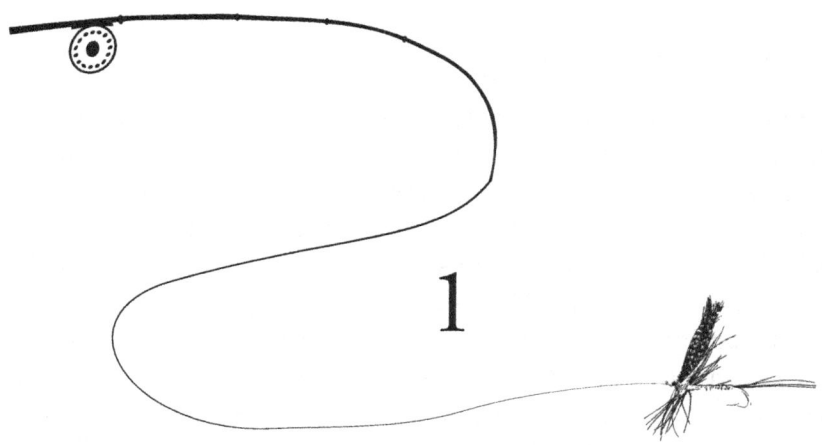

# 1

## McSherry's Saloon

The fishing flies I tie catch trout and salmon. For that reason, some few people know my name: Theodore Gordon. These few, city-bound anglers, chilled from a day hurrying icy sidewalks, withdraw to their studies and open their fly boxes. Conjuring spring's warm breezes and forest floors fragrant with blooming trillium and spring beauty, they study each compartment, pausing over the empty ones. The missing flies remind them of lost trout. They see the struggling fish, and they see their line part. Then they remember me, the fly tier, and start a list, Gold Ribbed Hare's Ears, Light Cahills, Dark Cahills, Wickham's Fancies, Tup's Indispensables, Parmachene Belles, Queen-of-the-Waters, Pink Ladies, Cardinals, Red Quills, Coachmen, and so many others.

It is January, three months before the 1915 trout season opens in New York. My mail arrives every day with more fly orders than I can handle. And so my backlog grows. The weather is to blame. The Catskills' freezing winter winds numb my fingers. On the coldest days, instead of tying flies, I lie abed under comforters scratching letters to warmer climes: Mary, George Noble, and others, in Savannah. Savannah. Warmer days, long past. The solicitous care of Anson Knight and his wife, Jeanie, here in Bradley, can never evoke those days. Simmering beef stews, pork roasts, freshly baked bread, and bleached sheets ensure survival. Nothing more.

Tonight, her work done, Jeanie Knight allowed me the run of her kitchen. Alone in the silence, I turn up the kitchen lamp and poke more wood into the stove. The warmth limbers my fingers, and they deal out fly tying materials on Jeanie's kitchen table: mailers, pens, Hall's hooks, scraps of muskrat, fox and mink fur, stripped peacock herl, silver tinsel, Hare's ears, gold wire, wood duck flank feathers, red ibis flight feathers, ginger and dun hackle, starling wings, and a curlew skin. And along with this lifeless mass, I set out my what-could-have-beens and the whys, bothersome regrets I cannot banish. The finished flies drop one by one into mailers. The regrets pursue me. A stiff back, I stand, stretch, and add more wood to the stove.

Before she left for her Class Meeting, Jeanie cautioned me, "No smoking in the kitchen, please, Mr. Gordon. The ash gets into my pie dough." The back porch lies outside her rules. So, I step into the night, roll, light, and draw in the familiar taste. The craving dies as my lips press the cigarette's thin paper and feel the quivering column of smoke beneath. I stretch again, and arching my back, I look up. Every star is visible and each of that myriad shines absolutely and distinctly in the mountain air. They appear so near. I take another puff and lift my burning cigarette to join them, its glowing tip, one more speck of light in a sky full of burning flecks spread out over heaven's vault where every shade of dark finds its place. Starlit Catskill nights are so bright that following deer and fox tracks requires little skill. Their trails stand out against the sparkling snow like *gesso* on white plaster walls. A mincing line of prints descends to the Neversink, fifty yards away. A fox stalking a foolish wandering grouse.

Jeanie's Class Meeting breaks up two houses down. The last hymn,

*As the darkness deepens O'er us, Lo! Eternal stars arise;*

*Hope and faith and love rise glorious, Shining in the spirit's skies.*

I catch the goodbyes and hear the approaching crunch of Jeanie's boots until her lone, pale shadow emerges into the starlight. A large, bulky woman, the starlight transforms her. Her shadow is thin and appears to glide over the snow as though the prayers and hymns have worked the impossible, trimming her great mass, leaving her as slender as one of my silver hackle feathers.

"There you are, Mr. Gordon," she says, knocking her boots against the bottom stair.

"Good evening, Mrs. Knight," I reply. "Sounds as if your meeting went well," I offer, needing her kitchen a few more hours.

"The meetings are always good. There is that moment on nights like this when the meeting and the heavens become one in me. It is only then I know, for certain, my place."

With difficulty, more difficulty than I anticipated, I say, "I have never been to a Class Meeting." She glances up. My insincerity noted.

"I must get you to one," she says and then, eyeing me suspiciously, adds, "You would find it…calming."

My glibness balks again, and all I can manage is, "Perhaps," not wishing to extend this conversation. "I'll need your kitchen a bit longer, Mrs. Knight."

"Take all the time you need, Mr. Gordon. The wood box is full of kindling. When you're done, throw the newspapers I've laid out into the fire."

"Of course," I said.

"Oatmeal in the morning." With that she stepped into her kitchen and, slowing, climbed the stairs to Anson's warmth.

I coughed and spat down the porch steps. A red splash on the sparkling white brought to mind a cold January night on the Bowery more than twenty years ago. It was a few years after I left Savannah and started working at my uncle's Wall Street firm. Of the many pleasures New York offered, my choice was walking the Washington Market for fly tying materials. Following one such shopping trip, I stood at McSherry's bar sipping warm ale. On the floor beside me was a sack with a whole Wood Duck and a

Plymouth Rock rooster. The rooster neck held some fine, small grizzly hackles colored a warm shade of brown.

McSherry's was a long, narrow room dedicated to the business of drinking. A polished mahogany bar and massive matching mirror ran down half its length. The only light, a few gaslight sconces that McSherry kept turned down. Just enough light to signal a waiter. The ale was creamy, and tonight there was a surprise. Music. An Irish group, a father and three sons, playing penny whistle, drum, and mandolin. The father, an aged tenor, sang in a voice roughened by smoky country pubs and shots of whiskey. His accent was impossible. Ill at ease, they played on a raised platform in the rear. Through the tobacco haze, I stared. The music was sad but vigorous.

"McSherry's relatives just over from Omagh," the bartender said without prompting. He pointed at my mug. "Refill?" The bartender, Gene, a McSherry fixture, was slight and balding with eyes aglow from a long day of tippling. McSherry never minded so long as the tipplers drew the customers' pints carefully.

"Yes," I said. "Thank you for the reminder, Gene. One more before the ferry to West Haverstraw."

"It'll be a cold ride tonight. You'll need a fortifier," he said with a smile.

Pausing for a moment, I said, motioning to the Irish musicians, "They're a rather glum lot."

"The wife and mother died on the boat over. She was a lunger, too weak to sleep on deck," the bartender replied. "I don't know how they believed she could make it past Ellis Island's doctors. It's a miracle the husband and sons were certified, but by then she slept beneath the waves."

I stared some more. The music brought some clapping above the drone of conversation. I coughed. Turning away from the bar, I coughed into my handkerchief, leaving a scarlet wad plainly visible in the snow-white linen even in McSherry's lamplight.

"You're not a lunger?" More an accusation than a question. The bartender paused, looking at me carefully.

Recovering and putting my handkerchief away, I said gruffly, "Gene, you should know better. Just a winter cold."

Gene was skeptical. "Don't get testy. I worry about my customers," he replied and then moved off to answer a call.

Picking up my sack and pewter mug, I moved closer to the music. Passing tables of workmen dressed in dungarees, blood-soaked aprons, and greasy coats, I found an empty table in the shadows near the stage. The blood on my handkerchief was brighter tonight. Over the last month, I noticed small flecks of red, but I dismissed them, preferring to think they came from a raw throat. But tonight was different. The blood was too thick to be ignored. It was then I thought of the sons on McSherry's stage and the shame of being a "lunger's" son.

The music started up again. After a fast jig, the father turned back to his sons and barked the next piece. All three sons looked up anxiously. One asked, "Do you really want to sing that tonight?" Without answering, the father, a gaunt man, looked up and, snapping his fingers, began the beat. His blazing eyes glared at the ceiling as if the stamped tin scrollwork taunted him. The drum began a regular beat and then dropped in volume when the penny whistle rose, tracing the opening notes of the tune. And finally, the mandolin joined in, elaborating all and introducing the tenor.

Staring out on the upraised faces of McSherry's regulars, the father began in a husky voice with each word hanging distinctly on his inner feelings,

*I wish I was in Carrickfergus*

*Only for nights in Bally Glen*

*I would swim over the deepest ocean, the deepest ocean to be by your side*

*But the sea is wide and I cannot swim over*

*And neither have I wings to fly*

*I wish I could find me a handy boatman to ferry me over to my love and die.*

The tenor choked and his eyes rolled again to the ceiling, transfixed. His mouth was working but no words sounded. A hush fell. The mandolin player marked time bringing the tune round to where the father could begin again.

*These childhood places bring sad reflection*

*Of happy days spent so long ago.*

*My boyhood friends and my own relations have all passed on like the melting snow.*

*I will spend my days in endless roving."*

The father squinted through the smoky haze struggling to continue. He failed and the mandolin player took over again and, after a run, brought the tune back to his entrance.

The sons were in great distress. But the father righted himself and began:

*Ah to be home now in Carrickfergus*

*On the long road down to the salty sea.*

*With gold and silver I did support her.*

*I'll sing no more 'til I've had a drink.*

*I'm drunk today and rarely sober."*

The silent audience began to rustle and with upraised mugs saluted. Not a word. Not a cheer. Just dozens of pewter mugs shining in McSherry's gaslights. The father nodded and looked down at his empty, trembling hands. So many absent faces crowded the saloon. Mothers, fathers, brothers, sisters, lovers, friends, all… all left back home across the treacherous Atlantic.

*A handsome rover from town to town.*

*Ah but I am sick now, and my days are numbered.*

*Come all you young men and lay me down.*

With that, the music ended abruptly, and the sons gathered about their father, supporting him as he slumped to his knees. "That'll be al' fer t'night," the drummer shouted in a thick brogue. The flash of coins lobbed onto the stage continued for a few minutes. The sons picked them up, bowed, and led their father away. Shortly, conversation rose again and all returned to the business of drinking.

That night on the ferry ride home, I, a lunger, and the son of a lunger, looked out across the starlit Hudson as it carried ice floes down to the Atlantic. I should have thought myself lucky to be alive but did not. Instead, I craved the tenor's devastation and a quick end to coughing up my lungs.

Nothing has changed.

## 2

## Dinner with Mrs. Henderson

"Mr. Gordon!"

It was Ann, Mrs. Henderson's Irish maid, a slim, long-limbed strawberry blonde with a face full of freckles. Her crisp gray and white uniform rasped when she cupped her hands to shout again, "Mr. Gordon."

"Heard you the first time," I muttered. My attention was on the surface of a deep pool off the Henderson's front yard. Mrs. Henderson claimed every trout feeding there because the pool was what remained of a mill dam and tannery put up by a grandfather decades earlier. After his death and at her direction, the tannery was torn down and moved from the Neversink to Brooklyn. And in what had been the tannery yard, up went her country house, a Dutch Colonial white frame, now brushed gold by the late afternoon June sun.

Mrs. Henderson took no chances. A sweet fragrance drifted off a dozen flower beds set among graveled walks where once the stench of tanning leather gagged passers-by. A show place now for clients.

"Did you say something Mr. Gordon?"

"Yes," I drawled and then fell silent.

"Be fair, Mr. Gordon. What did you say?"

"I said I heard you."

"Will you join Mrs. Henderson for supper?"

"Not if I don't catch the entree," I muttered again.

"What did you say Mr. Gordon?"

Rise rings disturbed the usually placid pool. I rang the colors, three differently colored flies and then a fourth which brought a splash, a powerful run, and a leap. A dark colored two pound brown trout. I beached it off the gravel riffle below the pool. Next came a noisy riser. Another splash and run. This time the fish hugged the bottom for a time but pressure and patience brought it ashore. A little less than two pounds.

"What did you say Mr. Gordon?" Ann shouted.

Mrs. Henderson stood up from weeding a flowerbed bordering the house. I had not noticed her there. A tall, shapely woman with a sharp mind and tongue to match. Sweeping back her black hair with her forearm, she glared at me. "Mr. Gordon! Where is that gentleman you pretend to be?"

Turning to Ann, she said, "Relieve Mr. Gordon of my fish and take them to cook!"

"Gladly, Ma'am." I waded ashore and handed over my creel. Head high Ann marched the graveled path to the kitchen.

Mrs. Henderson turned to me, "Supper in an hour. The summer kitchen has water and a basin for you to wash up. Take off your wading shoes! You shall not mark up my new wood floors! Ann will find slippers for you. "

"Where's Sam?"

"Mr. Henderson's in the city. We're designing a new line of luggage and some of the drawings were not to my satisfaction."

Dinner alone with Mrs. Henderson, a dreadful prospect.

"When you've cleaned up, Ann will guide you to the sitting room."

The hand that decorated the Henderson sitting room showed a studied nonchalance, waxed pine board floors, hooked rugs, a field stone fire place and tall casement windows with deep wells. Sitting face-to-face in wing back chairs, Mrs. Henderson and I sipped sherry from stemmed crystal glasses. Candle light and a slight fire dispelled the chill and the shadows creeping in from the Neversink.

Setting the agenda for our conversation, Mrs. Henderson began, "Mr. Henderson left a few questions for you. To his list I have added my own."

"Are you an angler?" I asked. Hoping my sarcasm did not bear too sharp an edge.

"I have been." Her eyes flashed with irritation.

"Did your father teach you?"

"Must it always be a man to instruct a young girl in field sports?" She made no effort to hide her hostility. No matter. Sam Henderson took my fly suggestions without argument, a dozen at a time. An evening with Mrs. Henderson was a small price to pay for his loyalty.

Savannah taught me the art of adroitly trying another's patience. Paired with a disagreeable dinner companion, I could go for hours exasperating them. Toying with Mrs. Henderson had its limits. And truth be told, I was out of practice after years in the Catskills where the quality of a truth was tested by the pain left from the telling. Tonight would prove painful no doubt. To have had this conversation in Savannah would have been my preference. There, it was impolite to get too near the naked truth.

So keeping my voice neutral, I asked, "Who was your mentor?"

"Lady Gertrude Campbell. We met when I accompanied my father to Britain to study their leather works. Lady Campbell persuaded him to leave me behind for a season. It was before her divorce from that hideous man."

"Her book is...a...charming." More sarcasm not lost on Mrs. Henderson.

Her eyes flashed. "Unlike you I learned fishing from my mentor rather than from her book. Lady Gertrude and I fished ponds for carp and chalk streams for trout. I forgive you, knowing that you first learned fly fishing from Norris' book rather than the man himself."

"You have me at a disadvantage Mrs. Henderson. I've never traveled to England." Ann and her freckles grinned from the shadows.

"Time for dinner Mr. Gordon. Bring your glass! We'll finish it in the dining room." Mrs. Henderson nodded to Ann, her cue to leave for the kitchen.

The dining room, more studied nonchalance. A long oak trestle table waxed and polished. A sturdy pine hutch and matching sideboard weighed down with Delftware platters picturing windmills and skating scenes, plates and cups with castles and horsemen. Burning candles, the only light but for the setting sun, sat in ornate Delft candlesticks. A room and table of blues and whites.

Mrs. Henderson stood behind the chair at the head of the table and motioned me to take the chair on her right. Before taking my seat, I held Mrs. Henderson's chair for her. "Thank you, Mr. Gordon. You do show flashes of gentlemanly conduct. A month under my direction would make you a polished gentleman."

Off guard, I said, "I am sure."

Ann placed a pile of *Fishing Gazette*s on Mrs. Henderson's left," Thank you Ann." Turning to me she said, "You might consider a trade. I could tutor you in manners, while you tutor Mr. Henderson in fly-fishing."

"Yours would be the more arduous task, Mrs. Henderson. No gentleman would force such an unfair bargain on a lady."

Mrs. Henderson pointed to the magazines and said, "My research on you, Mr. Gordon. Before launching into my questions, let me correct one egregious mistake you've made in print more than once." Mrs. Henderson put her hand on the stack of *Fishing Gazettes*. "You write of boiling trout. No serious chef boils trout unless making fish stock. A chef poaches fish. The water never comes to a full boil. It simmers. Do you see the distinction?"

"I believe I do." Stymied by Mrs. Henderson's bluntness, I side stepped her lesson, "Not wanting to rush you, shall we start on Sam's questions." Ann set out platters of new potatoes, asparagus, and buttered peas. She brushed against me and rustled with purpose spreading the sweet scent of lilies of the valley. Then she presented the platter of trout. I looked up, and she smiled down at me seeking approval. I smiled back.

Mrs. Henderson would never seek my approval, and I resented her for it. Wealthy, educated, and well-traveled, all the things I was not. "Mr. Gordon, I will get to Samuel's questions after you've answered mine."

She opened a *Fishing Gazette*. "Before starting in, let me praise your writing style. As a writer you sound the diffident amateur, very British, conversational in tone, what passes for educated discussion in London men's clubs."

An unpleasant evening stretched before me. Mrs. Henderson and I were at cross-purposes. She wanted clarity; I abhorred it. Clarity comes easily to those lacking experience. For those with experience, there is only wit.

'But let me return to your *Gazette* articles. I marvel at the nonsense you write. "In one stream here," you write, an insect hatches out in May, "large and fat, light in color." You avoid identifying the insect, the stream, the hook size and the fly tying materials needed to dress it, all matters any passionate angler would want to know.'

I retreated into silence rather than provoke open conflict.

Mrs. Henderson looked up, her gray eyes coloring darker as she gazed at me. "Nothing Mr. Gordon."

"Artificial flies have no more longevity than the insects they imitate."

"Why not say that Mr. Gordon instead of leading us into trivia." Shuffling through the pile of *Gazette*s, she pulled out another issue, "Yes. Here you wrote how you forgot a box of dry flies which imitated a hatching mayfly of "peculiar" color, "a sort of fleshy dull yellow below and speckled fleshy legs." No size mentioned, the stream unnamed, and no recipe offered for tying the imitation. You never fished the flies because you left them in your dresser. Nonetheless you wrote the pattern would have enticed the largest trout." Fixing me, she raised her voice, "How do you know that? Are you a crystal-gazer?" When I hesitated, she charged ahead, "Pure speculation."

Shuffling through the stack again, she picked up another issue and smiled to herself, 'You wrote that, "Lake fishing is different…" and then, purposefully, did not describe the difference. I know the difference because Lady Campbell schooled me in the difference. And perhaps you know the difference but it's clear you didn't want to share your knowledge with your readers. Later you shamelessly summed up a series of contradictory angling accounts with the profound…let me underscore "the profound" aphorism, "Many men, many minds." She glared at me, "You can do better than that. Instead you've developed a talent for cloaking essential details. Revealing but not too revealing. I doubt if anyone caught a fish based what they read in any of your articles. You certainly did not intend their success. You are a shameless self-promoter. All you want is to put your name before the public, and that, I will acknowledge, you did achieve. It is as much the *Gazette's* fault as your own. It paid you for misdirection."

Raising my hand to object, she hushed me, "Please spare me your evasions. We have more ground to cover."

"If you prefer, I'll sit here quietly."

"Yes." Reading from another *Gazette,* she looked up her eyes flashing. 'Here is a gem. "Rainbow," you write, are found in "a large, bold stream such as you would call a river." In late season they "ascend tributary brooks." Are you writing about a river or a stream that could be called a river? More importantly you make no mention of which "maybe" river or tributary brooks hold rainbow.'

"You are doing doing nothing more than proving your poor opinion of me," I offered, my voice neutral.

'The evidence against you supports my opinion. Your own words convict you." She pulled out another *Gazette,* "More gems! You wrote about strange incidents involving frogs gorging on their young, ocean fish kept in fresh water, and how the song of the katydid marks the first day of the six weeks leading to fall. These accounts were all published. You even won approval for such nonsense as, "Fly-making is a fascinating amusement…" From what I have seen in Mr. Henderson's fly box, fly tying is something you are well qualified to write about yet never an article from you on the subject."

"I appreciate the compliment. Many good books teach fly tying. Anything I write would be superfluous," I said.

"So you say, but we will never know will we?" She fixed me sternly and after a pause went on, 'In a 1903 piece you described a fly that was not "of much service, except for a short time in 1898." Dated information. No explanation and no dressing offered. Of what use is this information?'

It was not a question which begged an answer so I remained silent.

Taking note of my silence, she said abruptly, "I will stop soon." Relieved, I sat back and waited, feigning composure. 'Your recent pieces are no more forthright. Secrecy remains your habit of mind. Last year you wrote, "In one small lake large fish were continually leaping at dragonflies, moths and butterflies…it was often desirable or necessary to have a good imitation in color and size…" You never thought to name the lake or the colors and sizes of the insects and, of course, you never described the dressings of the flies you used.'

"The lake was remote," I replied.

Miffed she growled, "I have one more. You invented and tested a fly on an unnamed bass river. You took more than a hundred fish in one day. There's no doubt bass fishermen would like the name of the river and the details of the fly, but you intentionally left those out. In the end you made a plea for 'common sense and reasonable, considerate action for humanity.' Your plea was heartfelt, I am sure," she said, lapsing again into sarcasm. "But more importantly, it gave nothing away. Your reputation as a gentleman angler remained intact while feeding the fraud at the same time."

"Mrs. Henderson, I sense you dislike me."

Alert, she sat back, eyeing me carefully, running the tip of her tongue deliberately over her lips.

"Why?" I asked.

"I am surprised you have not already guessed. Your business is assisting businessmen shirk theirs. Instead of Samuel worrying about our new luggage line, he worries about fooling trout. And he thinks you have the answers."

"My father and grandfather were successful during the Civil War when our company outfitted the Union cavalry with saddles and such. Profits are harder to come by these days. Fewer army contracts. We need new markets. More people are traveling, and they need luggage. They are our new market. Mr. Henderson does not feel the urgency I do, and you are the reason for his disinterest. Instead of planning the manufacture of attractive pieces of luggage, Samuel dreams of whipping the Neversink for trout," she gestured to the platter of poached trout. "Cook can purchase those for a few quarters when our taste runs to trout."

"Harmless enjoyment."

"Enjoyment, yes. Harmless, no. You lead Samuel and businessmen like him back to their boyhood. Little boys don't build great businesses. I am afraid Samuel will, with your help, get stuck in the past. And what is more, you corrupt not only grown men but you've engaged in much worse."

"Hardly."

"You are corrupting young men. One is that nice young man at the post office. Roy?"

"Yes, Roy Steenrod."

"And another is the young man who makes deliveries here. Ann is quite taken with him. He cuts quite a figure. Christian?"

"Yes, Herman Christian."

"I hear there are others. All waiting for the sound of your flute to lead them into the highways and byways, itinerant fly fishers like yourself, earning their way taking odd jobs and tying flies."

"I have become what I now am, having little choice in the matter."

"Are you one of those dour Scots Presbyterians who justifies his immorality by claiming Predestination?"

"My mother advised me not to discuss religion, politics and money in polite society. I believe you are a member of polite society."

"It appalls me you are so useless."

"Are you done now, lady?" My stoic face slipped, "Let's get on with Sam's questions."

"There is more, but I will show mercy."

"No need. You've missed the point of my *Gazette* articles. They promote the United States as an inexhaustible, public fishery for trout and salmon. A land so vast the average British angler cannot grasp it. In the *Gazette,* I'm the congenial travel writer selling our rivers and lakes. The British need not know the names of our rivers and flies. What they need to know is what they are missing."

"That had occurred to me, but I dismissed it. Your articles in *Forest and Stream* are similarly vague. No, Mr. Gordon, you're impossibly secretive. Worse, you pretend to care about your readers, when in fact you purposely leave them as ignorant as they were before they read your pieces."

"No changing your mind I see. By the way, the poached trout was perfectly cooked as was the asparagus with the Hollandaise sauce." I chewed slowly while Mrs. Henderson ate distractedly consulting her notes. "As you request, I will now move onto Mr. Henderson's questions. The first is straightforward. Which flies do you fish?" Mrs. Henderson turned to Ann, and Ann handed her a notebook and pen.

"The Gordon Quill, the Gordon, both Cahills, Coachman, Royal Coachman, Leadwing Coachman, Wickham's Fancy, Pale Evening Dun, the American Grannom, and the Beaverkill."

"All dry flies...?"

"All can be fashioned to float..." Sam was reading Halford and ordered only dry flies.

The scratching stopped, "You've given me eleven, but you fish other patterns."

"True. I tie experimental patterns which have no name."

"Secret all?"

"Private, I prefer. I'm testing them and so can't recommend them until they prove worthy.

"Would you let me look through your fly boxes?"

"No."

"So you've given me a list, a list, by the way, any tackle store clerk could provide me. And you sit here and expect me to report to Samuel these eleven flies are the flies you fish."

"To clarify, these are the named flies I fish...among others."

Mrs. Henderson shook her head slowly, "We are getting nowhere. Secrets and lies. That's what you're made of Mr. Gordon." She turned again to her notes saying, "We will plow ahead. When do you fish?"

"Whenever I can get out."

"No time of day is better than any other?"

"I prefer evenings. The best time to be out is whenever large trout are feeding. I cannot tell you more."

"You cannot or you will not?"

Her staring gray eyes made me uncomfortable. "That's the best I can do for you,"

I replied not wanting to lose Sam as a customer.

Her last question came out in a hiss, "What is the most important piece of advice you can offer Samuel?"

"Change flies frequently until you find the fly the fish will take. When you find the right fly, keep fishing it."

"I could give him that priceless piece of wisdom myself," she spat out. Surveying me, she asked, "What about fishing the fly that imitates the natural on the water?"

"Good advice as long as the artificial gives the same effect on the water as the natural."

"Effect?"

"Yes. Don't imitate the natural in your hand. Rather find the fly that simulates the aspect of the natural on the water." As an afterthought, I added, "Just the other day I fished a Wickham's Fancy during a caddis hatch. In the hand it looked nothing like the natural but sitting on the water it matched it perfectly. I caught fish." This was enough. Shutting my mouth firmly, I wondered if I had offered too much. Reviewing what I said, I decided it was more than enough to keep Sam as a customer. Any more would have been a bad bargain.

"You surprise me, Mr. Gordon." She pushed the pile of Fishing Gazettes aside and said, "In spite of yourself, you betrayed sincerity just now." She sat back eyeing me coldly, turning my words over carefully. Finally, "Dessert?"

Over rice pudding, Mrs. Henderson spoke of the weather, the accommodations at the Trout Valley Inn, and the impolite anglers who fished past her yard, "as if they owned it. They neither wave nor offer a thank-you." She was considering posting her property. "That will put an end to their rudeness."

Finally stifling a yawn, she said, "Ann, show Mr. Gordon to his room."

Ann led me to a narrow room off the kitchen. A servant's room. A single bed, chair, and chest of drawers left me little room to even turn around. Crowded, the same way Jeanie Knight makes me feel.

# 3

## Jeanie Knight's Secret

As is his nightly routine, Anson Knight damps down the kitchen stove before going to bed. I hear the squeak and his heavy steps on the stairs. By degrees the house grows colder until my uncovered hands and nose sting. Cringing, I pull my blankets up over my face and burrow my hands beneath. The only sound is Jeanie's kitchen clock as it ticks ponderously, an emphatic reminder of life passing, my own oscillating internal gears, the inhalation and exhalation of lungs, the ebb and flow of artery and vein, the to and fro of striving and failing. Moment by moment, my waking present sounds, then dies, hemorrhaging into the past. Each swing of my gears individual, each swing unique, the last swing absolutely destined. Then, me, gone for good. The kitchen clock does not know that moment. Only my heart knows it. And when questioned, it teases me like an abandoned wife. "You have ignored me too long," it says and then cackles, "You cannot be trusted." I refuse to play its game, and it punishes me with apprehension.

In the dark my most terrible fears ambush me. Lack of money, ill health, memories of my failures, memories of my cruelty and now my most terrible fear, my fear of Jeanie. Yes, I fear Jeanie Knight. She tracks my decline, precipitous of late. No one else notices. It had been my secret and my secret alone, or so I believed. But when Jeanie began indulging me in small ways, I realized she discerned my secret. She believes me near death. For certain my death is not far off. Of that my doctors have warned me. But how far off is it? Of that they and I are not sure. Jeanie believes it imminent. And it irritates me that she does. So I refuse to acknowledge her small kindnesses for fear I could also be seen confirming her suspicions.

In reflective moments I berate myself for becoming careless, for believing Jeanie's quiet patience betrayed mental torpor. My guard down, I expected her to lose her way in the ambiguity of my past, the stuff I spin into all manner of speculation for the people of Liberty. Instead she shows no interest in it, never trying to pin me down as others do when I make purposefully vague biographical references. She does not even try to unearth the carefree boy I hid away. Perhaps she understands, as I have long understood, that I have forgotten that boy. The passage of years made him and his open delight in the day a stranger to me.

From the day Anson and I struck terms, Jeanie knew I was a consumptive. With the Loomis Sanitarium nearby, local people recognize consumption's signs. Many townspeople care for the "winter boarders," the consumptives who arrive for the winter months to breathe the sterile mountain air. My mother is one. So long as the winter boarders pay regularly, do not cough in housekeepers' and waiters' faces, and do not spit on the floor, their disease is overlooked. Some winter boarders grow stronger and go back to the city to pick up the threads of their lives. Some do not and die here. I will never be going back to the city. This is my third straight year of coughing blood. My heart has weakened. The mountain cure no longer works. And my doctors know of no other.

Instead of dwelling on my decline, I fix my mind on April 3, 1915, Opening Day, the day trout fishing starts up again in New York. I am determined to survive the months until then, for I hope to gain new strength in the spring days that follow. A thrashing fish sending a jolt up my line, the warmth of full sunshine in the meadows, moist breezes, and easy walking over spongy turf. Just what my lungs need to heal; just what I need to breathe deeply. Just what I need to live another year.

Single minded, Jeanie clings to her conviction. And nothing I do distracts her. Like an opera manager, I searched backstage storage cupboards from my Savannah and Wall Street days to discover a forgotten costume, some overlooked character. I did come across one, the sophisticated gentleman traveler. Our every conversation now begins with "Mrs. Knight" or "Madam," expecting such civilities to distance me from her. They do not. Embellishing this role, I find fault with her whenever our paths cross. Gentlemen, especially Southern gentlemen, expect servants to know their place.

I make sure all our encounters begin with a formal demand, the sort of demand which reminds Jeanie she is my servant. To my surprise she quickly saw through me and has become preternaturally patient during our encounters. I realized then that the thought she was my servant never crossed her mind. Stolidly, her face expressionless, she repulses subjugation even though I persist. I cannot beat her down. She looks at her hands hearing me out and then looks up blandly, "Of course, Mr. Gordon." And I know she is thinking, "He's dying. I'll be kind to him in his last days." In her mind we are on equal footing, two human beings working out their days in close proximity to each other, nothing more than a knowledgeable nurse showing compassion for her cranky old patient.

Without discussing it, Jeanie and I now share a great unspoken truth. Perhaps the greatest truth of my existence. We know that we both know that I am declining and that death is not far off. I cannot predict how long this truth will remain unspoken between us. It is an uneasy truce. Nor can I predict how long it will be before others learn my secret and find me pitiable. Living in a state of prolonged anxiety, I stalk about the house, stubbornly apart. I am sharing my deepest truth with a woman I truly do not know, and even more disturbing, a woman I choose not to know. I want to think of her as an ill-educated, country woman whose only worth is managing a boarding house. A maid, a cook, a laundress. Nothing more. To think of her any other way raises complications I am not prepared to face. Thus I spend each day living in fear, fear of her pity and fear of the pity of those she might tell of our secret.

So I ridicule her. Referring to her as the "fat lady" always draws a laugh. My visitors smirk at my much inflated tales of her tippling my bourbon alone in the kitchen. The tales are fictitious. Only once did I see her take a swallow. And then it was at my invitation. No one bothers to ask why I am hostile to the one person who shows me unfailing kindness. In fleeting moments of self-honesty, I too am dismayed at the depths of my hostility toward her. Her kindness infuriates me, and I do not understand why.

For the present, making fun of Jeanie's heft blunts the irritating thought of her interest in me. Now hardly a hundred pounds, I am steadily losing weight. Jennie, on the other hand, is a formidable presence, not so much fat as solidly muscular. She has no waist and her baggy house dresses hang shapelessly. She fills doorways and blocks stairways with her mass, but her mass has a purpose. She chops wood and butchers pigs. She wields a meat cleaver with the same effortless dexterity I handle a cheese knife. Nothing on her quivers when she pounds down a maul on a helpless block of frozen maple, driving the screech of rending wood to startle neighbors. Her strength points up my decline, so I mock her.

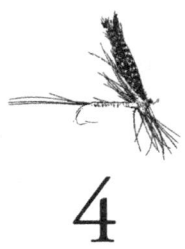

# 4

## Fly Tying

My mother indulged me as a child. Age twelve, she gave me Norris' *American Angler's Book*. And I discovered fly fishing and fly tying. The attitude of mind suited me. Throughout my young life, I traded in deception. Taking on guises, I lived a life of make-believe. Coached by my mother and uncles, I stowed away the ecstatic, thoughtless child who wandered the sunny pastures and teaming trout streams of Carlisle. This carefree boy was dangerous. When he showed signs of revealing too much, my mother brought him up short. "Get a hold of yourself," she commanded, "if you want to prosper." Thus, I learned to guard against my impulses and foster new personalities.

My guises flourished, all carefully drawn so none became irksome. At twelve, one guise preoccupied me above all. It was appearing as a healthy boy. I loathed my frailty, fearful others would see me for the sickly, pathetic child I was. Every morning, I woke doubting my hold on life. The rest of my day I spent distracting others from entertaining that same doubt. Appearing healthy became an obsession. Studying the signs of vigorous life, I faked them, presenting myself to the world as a vital, rugged boy. I talked fishing and hunting. I talked long mountain climbs and days afield in bad weather. I talked the way outdoors men talk, and some of my talk was even true. Most were fooled. They believed, as I wanted them to believe, that I was strong and lively.

And so fly tying fascinated me, each fly my life in miniature. To be effective, artificial flies must show signs of life. Poetic anglers have called artificial flies frauds. And so they are. The fraud comes in making lifeless feathers and pinches of fur appear alive. Just as with the rest of my life, tying flies challenged me to deceive. I became a prophet raising the dead to life, each fly a resurrection. In fly tying, the trick is always the same: to imitate life. I do not imitate the natural fly trout are taking. Rather, I imitate the life of the natural fly they are taking. Among my customers, the superstitious believe I impart a power to my flies. I do not discourage this notion because there is some truth to it. My flies appear alive to the fish and that illusion few of today's fly tiers work to impart.

Neatly at hand, a mallard skin, a hare's mask, and thin gold tinsel rest on my tying table. Mr. Granville Harman, a founding member of the Brooklyn Fly Fishers, wants a dozen Gold Ribbed Hare's Ears. "One more fly to go," I say under my breath, keeping the count. Cutting about twelve inches of black silk thread from a Pearsall bobbin, I draw it over a lump of tacky bees wax. The beeswax softened in a patch of sunlight on my windowsill. Only one size sixteen left to do, so a size sixteen Hall's hook goes into my vise.

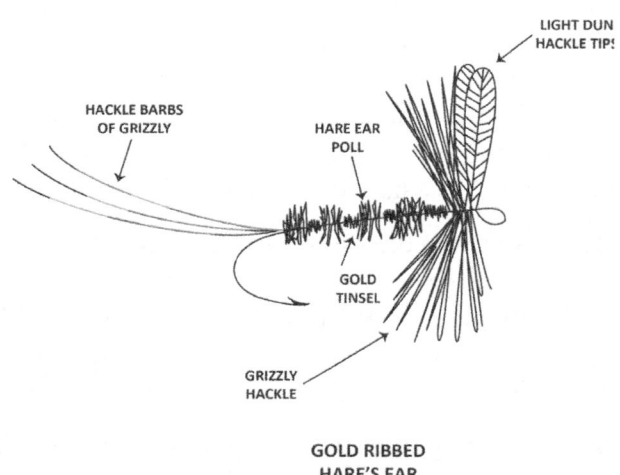

GOLD RIBBED
HARE'S EAR

I blow on my hands to warm them. It triggers a cough, and I spit. The news pages Jennie placed under my chair collect one more red splotch. I sit back marshaling my wavering energy and the memory of my first Opening Day as a fly fisherman. Mother allowed me to spend it at my uncle's Carlisle farm. After months of teaching myself to tie trout flies, the great day finally arrived to test them. Miserable weather. Shouldering my green hickory rod, I sneaked out at sunrise before my uncle and aunt woke.

Gusts of sleet drove me into their pasture, and without letting up, they prodded me down pasture rills to bigger and bigger water. Here and there crouching back from the water's edge, I dropped my flies in holes or along undercut banks, fishing them like worms. They swung lonely in the currents. I jigged them under logs and by boulders. It was discouraging. No takers. Months of reading and collecting fly tying material, months of tying flies by the book, each fly a prayer for success. My prayers went unanswered. I kept at it.

The air warmed, and the sleet turned into a warm drizzle. Looping on a Leadwing Coachman, a pattern Norris extolled, I had my first success. My concoction of copper-colored peacock herl and slips of storm-gray goose wafted down into a deep four-foot hole. Halfway down, a brilliant trout struck and missed. Encouraged, I offered it again and again as it fluttered and flashed in the currents. The second strike was sure, a brief flash and a stubborn pull. The fish hooked itself as it dove. Startled, I yanked, and there before me was a writhing brook trout, dark purple and black along its back, speckled blue and vermillion along its sides, and orange and cream lower down. My luck had changed.

The brook trout was drawn to the scattered light, I guessed, for that was what drew my eyes when watching my fly descend into the dark hole. Its glossy hackle barbs dispersed light like a prism even in the overcast. The flash of light was one sign of life making my fraud effective. There were others as I came to learn.

My Carlisle days guide me even today tying Hare's Ears for Mr. Harman. The traditional Hare's Ear pattern calls for a tail of grizzly hackle barbs. That is what my customers expect and that is what they get. So I tie shiny stiff grizzly hackle barbs cut from short feathers located along the edges of a cock's head, the spade hackles. For my own Hare's Ears, I use ginger hackles. Where speckled trout predominate, I tie my Hare's Ears with a red tail. A little red in a brook trout fly never hurts. This is especially true fishing mountain streams. No longer have I such ties in my box. Mountain fishing is behind me.

Mr. Harman expects his Hare's Ears' tails as long as the body. So that is what I tie for him. Aesthetically correct proportions are more a lure for anglers shopping for flies than for trout hunting a meal. The proportions demanded by the market were first enshrined by our art schools. They please the angler's eye as a painting might please their eye. Anglers have taken what they find aesthetically pleasing and raised it to an entomological law.

Nature does not concern itself with how its offspring appear. Rather, it shapes them to efficiently fulfill the functions they perform. A bumblebee's wings appear disproportionately small to its bulky body. It does not matter. They are the right size for what it does. Most mayflies' tails are longer than their bodies. Thus the barbs of its imitation should extend out behind the body as long as the tail of the mayfly. That is my rule. Mr. Harman, as with most anglers, has no insect in mind when he selects his flies. So he wants the tails of his flies proportionate to the length of the hook's shank. As the customer, that is what he gets.

The Catskills taught me nature's aesthetic norms. For years, I brought home bottles of insects preserved in alcohol. Mayflies, caddis, stoneflies, craneflies. They sit on my desk, and I study them from different angles and in different light. At first, our aesthetic norms blinded me to what my eyes saw. Finally, measuring the tails, bodies, wings, and legs of species after species, I saw how nature set its own norms.

My tying became, as so much of my life, two-faced. The flies I tie for clients observe mankind's aesthetic norms. The flies I tie for myself observe nature's. Another secret of mine I hesitate to reveal because my misshapen flies catch more and bigger fish. When tying for the market, the customer has the last word. They would never buy the flies I tie for myself. And so, in my vice, I begin spinning a double fraud for him.

My next strike came from under a log, a paper birch, last year's dead fall. The tree blocked the stream from bank to bank, and the current dug a deep hole beneath it. I knelt on the bank and lowered my fly, at the same time releasing several feet of line. Tightening as the fly slid under the tree trunk, I swam the Leadwing Coachman against the current, jigging it up and down. A powerful strike. I pulled hard, and then harder still, but the fish was stubborn. Excited, I pulled all the harder, and the line broke. I never saw the fish. Deflated, I noticed for the first time how chill the drizzle was. Sitting limp in the wet grass, I pulled up the end of the line. It was curled; the snell's loop had slipped.

Fragility is another sign of life I incorporate into my flies. Effective flies must appear ephemeral even to the point where the tier sacrifices durability. Thus I hoard, as all good tiers must, every wrap of thread. The bodies of natural mayfly duns and adult caddis are hardly greater round than a hook shank. So after securing the tail, I argue against each wrap. For Mr. Harman, as for most of the members of the Fly Fishers, I tie only dry flies, but with one adjustment, the short tails cant slightly up. If they did not, the hackle barbs would break the surface tension of the water, and the fly would sink. Thus for dry flies, I add a single extra wrap under the tail before wrapping the spade barbs. Mr. Harman expects durability, so I add an extra wrap or two and a drop of lacquer.

The body comes next. It is dubbed fur plucked from the ears of a hare, hence the name of the fly. Depending on the season, hares' ears carry different mixes of colors and can be tied lighter and darker. In truth, the Hare's Ear fly could be tied in any color from black, to gray, to brown, to an orange/yellow, to a white, and still be true to its advertising. Mr. Harman expects the darker summer phase. That is the standard tie. The ears are from hare I shot two summers ago. I stroke the coarse fur and feel the checkered stock of my Parker double barrel, a custom piece bought in Savannah during better times. I went out before sunrise to an abandoned farm.

Seated, my back resting against a decaying woodpile, I faced what had been the yard and waited. Sunrise, two hare circled sniffing and munching. As they neared me, one crossed in front of the other, and I caught both with a single shot. Even now picking up an ear, smiling, I can smell the cordite. Generous with her parsley, thyme, cloves, and peppercorns, Jennie cooked a delicious Hasenpfeffer. I supplied the red wine.

Short coarse fur plucked from the back of the hare's ears pile up on my knee. To it I add a pinch of long, soft gray fur taken from the hare's pelt. It will help bind together the short, bristling fur of the hare's ears when I spin it. After mixing the fur thoroughly into a jumble of unsorted browns, tans, whites, grays, and blacks so no one color dominates, I take a small pinch and spin it on the waxed thread with my thumb and forefinger creating a yarn. This yarn I wrap forward covering three-quarters of the hook shank. The yarn is more lightly spun near the tail and slightly heavier with each successive wrap. This gives a tapered look with the rear appearing slimmer than the thorax by about half. A convincing profile. Another sign of life.

Gold tinsel finishes the body. It is wound forward over the dubbing. It must be tightly wound, the wraps neither too close together nor too far apart. Too close, and they stifle the loft of the dubbing. Too far apart, and the body will not appear segmented. Segmentation—another sign of life. The bodies of most adult aquatic insects are segmented. When the fly is finished, I will pick out the dubbing from between the tinsel wraps to exaggerate the segmentation. Unless the tinsel is wound tightly, it will loosen when fur strands are freed up. The teeth of brown trout wreak havoc on loose tinsel. Peeking out from the hare's ear dubbing, the tinsel will wink yellow. A trout looking at a Hare's Ear from below will see flickering bursts of the gold and many other colors as from the inner glow of a transforming dun.

Fooling large trout with a well-tied artificial fly is not simply a matter of addition. Another quality is needed to join all together into a living ensemble. A single overriding quality must infuse all and enliven the fraud. That quality is randomness. It is the soul of the fly, and good tiers infuse each fly they tie with a soul. Thus for the Hare's Ear dry fly, I tie in fragility, the appearance of segmentation, tapered multicolored dubbing, flashes from gold tinsel, and flashes from glossy spade hackles. And all of these together and in balance foster a convincing fraud. One dominating element destroys the balance betraying the fraud. A few glossy spade hackle barbs support the fraud. Too many broadcast it. The same with gold tinsel, a greater temptation for the tier. Several twists heighten the fraud. Too many and the fly shows no more life than a gold ingot. Random flashes attract trout. Incessant flashes make them suspicious.

For wet flies like the Leadwing Coachman, occasional flashes are even more critical. Tumbling in the current, natural bugs wink as they swim, flip, and roll. The random flash catches the trout's attention. The sparkle of the spade tail comes and goes as do sporadic flashes from the peacock herl body. That and other random signs of life make the fraud tantalizing. A living lie—something I have worked my whole life to perfect.

My creel fills up. Dinner for my uncle and aunt assured, I experiment. Switching from pattern to pattern, about a dozen in all, I test the merits of each. None stands out so I finish off with a Great Red Spinner, a simple tie, red ibis for the tail, red mohair wound with gold wire for the body, brown mallard covert slips for the wings and a ginger-colored hackle. Good fly patterns never go out of style. The Great Red Spinner, a favorite of Norris, is still effective for brook trout in the headwaters of the Neversink.

Evening sneaked up on me in the gloom of the overcast. I turned back fishing up the pasture stream I had just fished down. It was easier going than coming. The rills colored as springs opened in the meadows dumping mud and last fall's leaves into the flood. Splashing through puddles, I leaped rivulets hunting for high ground. Sometimes I misjudged and fell short, up to my knees, soaked. At long last, twilight took pity, taming the drizzle to a fog carved by the wind into grotesque, milling specters.

My aunt's thick beef barley soup and fresh bread drew me on. The barley was soaking on her kitchen counter when I left in the morning. Perhaps a hot bath first. Out of the frayed mists, I heard my uncle's frantic calls. A disembodied sound rendered otherworldly by the lack of familiar landmarks. It was only when I saw his face I became frightened. He was cross.

"What is your mother going to say when you come down with pneumonia?"

Holding up my creel, I announced, "I caught dinner."

We stood staring at each other in the fog and cold. Momentarily, my uncle chuckled, then turned serious, "Brook trout can't cure pneumonia." After a warm bath, there was the soup, fried trout, and warm crusty bread.

Another cough. Again it shakes me. I mean to hold on until Opening Day. Good mountain air and long, leisurely walks will restore me for another year of piece work. It always has.

Tying in a grizzly hackle to simulate the insect's legs is the next step. Mr. Harman counts himself among the ranks of scientific anglers. He fishes his flies only on the surface. He wants his dry flies to float regardless of conditions. Thus, for Mr. Harman, I tie in two hackles. My high floating two hackle flies keep him satisfied.

The wings for the Hare's Ear come last. Norris attached the wings after tying in the tail, body, and hackle. I follow his congenial influence. Halford suggests the opposite, tying in the wings first instead of last. For a time, I followed his advice in this, as in other matters, but reverted in the end to Norris' method. His is faster and, more importantly, it requires fewer wraps of thread.

Wings come just behind the eye of the hook. My customers insist on paired wings. So I tie their flies with paired wings. When tying for myself, I add no more than a single wing for my own sparse flies. The problem in tying in two wings is balancing them. If the tier does not, the fly twists during the cast and alights either on its side or its back. And worse, it will snarl the leader, forcing the angler to replace it. Nature provides the balance. The guarantee is the full mallard skin. For Mr. Harman, I tie in balanced slips from a bird I skinned and cured myself. With slips from the same location on opposing wings, the fly will alight, wings up, cast after cast.

Through experimentation, I have found that no one feather makes a fly effective. Not wood duck, nor mallard, nor even starling. Some anglers swear that a dun hackle from the neck of a blue heron is a powerful attractant. To my mind, such a feather is at best one sign of life if the color is right. Other signs are needed and then only when all work together to deliver a convincing fraud.

For Mr. Harman, I rip out light dun strips from Mallard flight feather and place them together on my knee. Mr. Harman complains of poor eyesight, so I tie in the lightest dun shade. The height of the wings is again ruled by human aesthetics. Customers will only pay for mayfly wings tied fully upright as high as the body is long. For Mr. Harman, I follow this rule, for that is what he expects. Many mayflies sprout wings that slant back over their bodies. This is especially true of the large mayflies that come on midsummer. Thus for myself, depending on the species, I will tie some imitations with wings extending back beyond the bend of the hook.

Moving my left index finger and thumb up behind the eye of the hook, I pinch the two strips of duck feather together, holding them on the top of the shank. The curved sides of the strips face out. I do not think it matters whether the wings are tied concave or convex. But again, Mr. Harman expects convex, so I tie them convex. After pinching the Mallard slips down, I maneuver the thread onto the butts and under my fingertips. Then I tighten and add two more wraps, one in front and one behind the wings to fix them upright. Then a whip finish and another good lie in the telling. It is the fly he wants, not the best trout fly I can tie.

Real mayfly wings glow when shot through with light. No feather I know of, even young starling, achieves that affect. Often when tying imitations of mayflies for myself, I discard the standard, more or less opaque, wing materials. For my own Hare's Ears, I tie in light dun hackle tips. The play of light through the glossy stiff barbs gives the appearance of a naturally translucent wing, a particularly alluring sign of life. Translucency is hardly ever a problem with caddis flies. The wings of most are opaque. So my cache of bird skins very often yield the perfect match for imitating caddis. For the translucent wings of stoneflies, I tie in four long hackle tips.

The Hare's Ears for Mr. Harman will catch fish, recently planted fish, and maybe a few that overwintered unmolested on the private club water of the Brooklyn Fly Fishers. But they will not catch the fussy big brown trout that inspect and routinely reject the hundreds of aesthetically perfect flies floating over them on public water. So in my vise is a lie. More flies and more lies to follow. Nonetheless, I send Mr. Harman my hardly frauds and pocket his money order. He got what he wanted and so did I.

Now for the dry Quill Gordons. I lay out dun-colored hackles, lemon-tinted wood duck flank feathers, stripped peacock herl, and twelve hooks of assorted sizes. My fingers start in. I will not finish tonight, but I push myself to make a good start so Mr. Harman will have them for Opening Day. At the Hardenburg clubhouse, he will show them to his friends over whiskey and brag about my flies and the many fish they bring to his net. His praise is my best advertising. He will note my name at the beginning of all his fish stories. "I had on a small Quill Gordon and...." Or "I dunked my Gordon in kerosene and blew it dry, waiting until...." Or "I was using a little fly bought off Gordon one day out on the Willowemoc...." His stories always end with full creels.

The dressings for flies are now as ritualized as ecclesiastical incantations. For instance, my own Quill sells commercially with paired wings of wood duck flank feathers, often splayed. When I first invented the dressing, my Quill did sport a pair of splayed wood duck wings. Since then, I have found other feathers, such as Mallard flank feathers, just as effective so long as they are the right shade. For myself, under certain conditions, I even tie it without wings. For my customers, it is different. They expect two wood duck wings, so that is what I tie up. The dressing is so enshrined, I, its inventor, cannot change it.

Below is a Quill Gordon I tied for myself. It is a sparse tie with single swept back wing. The tail has a minimal number of dun hackle barbs. Note the few turns of dun hackle tied in before the wing *a la* Norris.

The last Quill Gordon for the night goes into a mailer. I lean back reflecting. Most years, Opening Day is an annoyance. Too many fishermen with too little regard for each other. They fish shoulder to shoulder, casting wildly, snagging each other's lines. They glare at their neighbors and stamp off muttering about stream ethics. Empty creels swinging, they splash from frigid pool to frigid pool in a blind fury, lashing the river, praying for a fish, any fish, even a six-inch brook trout to preserve their dignity. In desperation, a fly flipped into the mouth of a trickling feeder creek, and they have their six incher, one fish more than most of the flailing host. To the question, "How'd you do?," they draw themselves up and say truthfully, "One." Then they lie, "A twelve-inch native. I gave it to some kids." Earlier the six incher sailed into the woods, food for scavenging cats.

Evening, anglers join companions for whiskey, supper, and stories. The good cheer distracts from the raw day, and soon well-being swallows up their frustrations. The loss of a client, an increase in office rents, the last stormy session with partners fixed on finding fault for a bad month, a wife's need for a new summer wardrobe, for a second maid. All this unpleasantness anglers set aside as they set aside the disappointments of Opening Day. Instead, they look ahead, anticipating warmer days when mayflies cover quiet waters. Miniature fragile sails floating trout treacherous pools. Breathless, the angler hangs on the courage of the Iron Dun, the courage of the Blue Quill, the courage of pure beauty, floating briefly perfect, before being sucked down, forever struck off the surface of the river, off the surface of life. A wasteful show so much like the rest of an angler's life. The endless ceremonies of life's milestones, and all to show for it, vendor's smiles, a stack of bills, and perhaps a guest's respectful praise that all went off without a hitch. Short-lived triumphs interred in newspaper society columns and family albums.

In bed, the last story told and the last whiskey downed, they drowse. Their final thoughts are on their flies, each its own show of beauty cobbled together from other shows of beauty. Mallard wings cupped to land slushy northern ponds; glossy brown mink's fur flashing beside a mountain torrent; Scarlet Ibis ruffling their wings as they stalk shallow marshes for shrimp; white polar bear hair no less brilliant than the snow-covered expanse they wander; and so much more of life's beauty, dissected and dried. Arrested shows severed from a pumping heart. All frozen in time. Absolute. All tied on a hook with colored silk thread, primrose, crimson, olive, yellow, dun.

With these visions, anglers fall asleep smiling. And I with them. Tonight, my dreaded future slipped away; perhaps the beauty of my flies dispelled it. Perhaps. Or perhaps I am just too tired to think on what will become my eternal silence. In the morning, I will finish Mr. Harman's flies. A few more extravagant shows. Once they impressed Gail, but as time proved, not enough.

# 5

## Dinner with Mr. and Mrs. Henderson

"Mr. Gordon!"

"Mr. Henderson. Good to see you." Sam Henderson caught me studying a large brown trout slurping Blue Quill.

He was out of breath. "I wasn't sure whether it was you who fished past our place." He caught his breath before saying, "You should've stopped."

"Little light's left, and I have an appointment with a large brown trout." Pointing upstream I said, "Had my heart set on that trout rising next to the flat boulder splitting the head of the pool. It's feeding on Blue Quill spinners. In fifteen minutes it will be too dark to cast." The pool was bordered along its left side by a steep sloping bank of loose rock. The right side was a narrow beach of fine sand and gravel hemmed in by popple.

"Mrs. Henderson expects us."

"Go back! I'll join you when I'm done here."

"Would you mind if I watched?"

"Not at all." I did mind. But it would have created a mystery, and mysteries provoke curiosity. "Stand far enough back so I'm not conscious of your presence." What I meant was so far back you cannot see my fly.

Talking over my shoulder, I waded within casting distance of the fish. "Been out fishing Mr. Henderson?"

"Yes and I've had some luck today. A half dozen beautiful natives. One ten incher."

"What did you catch them on?"

"Dry flies of course. Following your advice, I've changed flies so often over the last few days I've forgotten what patterns were effective. Been to Mills and bought a dozen each of the flies you recommended except of course your Quill and the Gordon. I want those from you. Your Quill is still the best of them."

"Thank you."

"La Branche is putting me up for membership in the Anglers' Club."

"You'll enjoy the company."

I dropped my small Blue Quill with dubbed cream dun body at the head of the pool. It swept over the large brown trout. Nothing. All day the sky had been overcast, leaden colored clouds threatening rain hung so low they tempted me to reach up and touch them. Only a sliver of pink glowed upon the horizon. The dubbed Blue Quill showed lighter than the naturals on the river. A glassy bodied dark fly would take on the leaden pink atmosphere better. Searching my fly boxes, I found one with a dark quill body. Fresh and glowing. A sparse tie. On the river it would sit low in the water reflecting light the way the naturals did.

Casting to the rhythm of the big trout's rises, I dropped the fly just above its last rise. Two feet of drift. It disappeared, and I struck. The trout jumped as if stung, and then headed straight for me. I stripped in line. Seeing me, it turned back racing into the heavy water at the head of the pool where it sounded dogging the bottom. Stubbornly it resisted my efforts to move it, a stalemate broken only when the pressure of the hook angered it. The trout lifted and tore for me once again. More stripping of line, and again it turned speeding toward the flat boulder. I put on as much pressure as I dared, and the fish circled back. For a moment it came to the surface on its side, then righted itself slowly. I guided it to the gravel beach. When the brown sensed the water shallowing, it turned to go, but I dropped down to my knees behind it, and in its fright it skidded up on the shore flopping wildly.

"A trophy," shouted Henderson falling on it. "It must go three and a half pounds," he said holding it up.

"And then some." By then the light had left the river. Looking up, I stared long at a flight of Blue Dun spinners heading upstream and when they were out of sight, a chill descended with the dark. I quickly boxed my sparse Blue Quill.

After washing up in the summer kitchen without prompting, I met the Hendersons in their sitting room. They were drinking sherry. Ann offered me a stemmed glass from a silver tray.

Inclining my head in a faint bow, I murmured, "Thank you, Ann."

"You are improving, Mr. Gordon," said Mrs. Henderson.

Again I was wearing slippers. Crossing my legs I jiggled one on the tip of a toe.

"Stop that Mr. Gordon." Mrs. Henderson flushed with irritation. "I spoke too soon."

Standing by the door Ann hid a smile.

Sam came to my rescue. "You should've seen Mr. Gordon hook and play the large brown trout we're having for dinner. It was masterful."

Mrs. Henderson grunted, "I am sure."

Ignoring his wife, Sam went on, "I should learn to tie flies." Sam looked over to me for support.

I smiled encouragingly, "I could recommend some books and help you collect what materials you need to get started."

"That would be generous of you."

"Samuel, do you know what you'd be getting into?" His wife huffed.

"I believe so," Sam said.

"Mr. Henderson, you will not be filling our house with bits of dead animals. They smell and draw bugs. It only takes a few moths to ruin our woolens."

"We could box them up with moth balls."

"That's what I do," I said.

'Nothing cries "Last year's fashions" like the smell of moth balls."

"That's what sachets are for, I believe. A lavender sachet among your woolens will work wonders."

"You seem well informed on the tricks of women, Mr. Gordon."

"Mother's very knowledgeable about such things."

"Do you see much of your mother?"

"In Savannah, we lived together. Now summers we see each other occasionally. During the winter she travels to Liberty, and we stay the season at the Liberty House."

"A winter boarder?" Mrs. Henderson asked neutrally as she glanced at Sam.

"Yes. She's frail." The conversation entered a lull.

Sam had been sipping his sherry steadily, and to end the lull he emptied his glass in a gulp and said, "Time for dinner, Dear?" Ann hurried off to the kitchen.

This time Mr. Henderson sat at the head of the table with me to his right, and Mrs. Henderson sat opposite me. Ann laid serving platters of hot rolls, mashed potatoes and peas in the center of the table, with the fish platter in front of Mr. Henderson. Sam asked for his wife's plate and inquired whether she wanted brown trout or brook trout. "Two brook trout."

When Sam turned to me, I said, "I'll take one brook and a portion of the brown."

Mrs. Henderson opened the table conversation with, "Everyone thinks anglers are kind and gentle people when in fact they're just as bloodthirsty as any hunter. They kill fish, birds, minnows, worms, and all manner of fur bearing creatures. Don't you agree, Mr. Gordon?"

"I both hunt and fish so I am guilty on both counts. In my defense, however, let me argue for leniency by stating that it has been many years since I killed a worm."

"Take me seriously, Mr. Gordon. Anglers snuff out life with the same alacrity a hunter does. Isn't that true?"

"Anglers, if successful, get blood on their hands. We often talk of having a killing fly."

"You don't seem concerned with all the killing. Do you ever return fish after you catch them?"

"Yes, undersized fish. As I get older, my greatest pleasure is creeling smart, old trout. They're not as tasty but I follow nature's code. Foolishness should not be rewarded. Trout live by that code, and understand the consequences when they run afoul of it. I'm just another one of their predators with the herons, otters, and others."

Mrs. Henderson turned to me, "So you've interrogated trout about their code of conduct. You are the Compleat Angler."

"I have often observed their merciless pursuit of their own kind. It's quite normal in the stomachs of large trout to find smaller trout."

"What do you think Mr. Henderson?"

"I agree with Mr. Gordon."

"Have you ever thought about extending charity to one of the big old trout you catch?" She asked.

"Charity is a scarce commodity. I reserve it for Mother and my relatives. So many of my competitors would like to feast on my fly tying business. Mills for one," I said turning to Sam. "Charity to Mills would hasten my end?"

Mr. Henderson grew thoughtful while Mrs. Henderson continued, "My only conclusion from what you tell me Mr. Gordon is that fishing turns you into a beast of prey. You descend to living by the law of the jungle. Kill or be killed. Am I right?"

Seeing Ann on the edge of the candle light, I recited more to her than to Mrs. Henderson:

*Come live with me, and be my Love,*

*And we will all the pleasures prove*

*That valleys, groves or hills, or fields,*

*Or woods, and sleepy mountains yield.*

Flashing a smile at Mrs. Henderson, I said, "You can probably recite the rest. These are not the words of a beast of prey." My reward was Ann's smile from the shadows.

Mrs. Henderson remained remote. "Do fishermen always fall back on *The Compleat Angler* when cornered?"

"Am I cornered?"

Even Mrs. Henderson smiled. "I'll give you that art can transform our animal instincts and transport them to a higher plane."

It was Sam's turn, "Mr. Gordon, do you read much?

"Some, mostly fishing books and magazines. Mother passes along novels and poetry which she thinks I might enjoy. I rarely read them now. My eyesight is failing. When we lived in Savannah, I read what everyone in society was reading."

"Have you a favorite poet?" Mrs. Henderson asked skeptically.

"One Georgia poet I find quite good."

"Yes?"

"Sidney Lanier, a Confederate soldier, a consumptive, and later a professor of literature at Johns Hopkins University."

"Could you recite some for us?"

I hesitated my eyes traveling from Mrs. Henderson to Sam and back again to Mrs. Henderson, and then to Ann. Fully expectant Ann waited for me to begin.

"These opening lines from one of his poems plague me:

*O Age that half believ'st thou half believ'st,*

*Half doubt'st the substance of thy own half doubt,*

*And, half perceiving that thou half perceiv'st,*

*Stand at thy temple door, heart in, head out.*

It's apropos of our time. It comforts me to know at least one other feels as I do."

"What a tortured soul you must be, Mr. Gordon!" Was Mrs. Henderson's judgment.

"Certitude escapes me, Mrs. Henderson. I envy you yours."

"What is the temple your heart is in and head out?"

"Need I say I am of two minds on that? My heart longs to be living within a family, but my head tells me I must resign myself to living alone. There were opportunities earlier in my life but my half doubting my half doubts paralyzed me, and so I discounted the truth before my eyes until the good within my grasp seemed a deception."

"Sounds like a woman lost," Mrs. Henderson said.

"Yes. Something like that." I said tersely, relying on my silence to close off further discussion. In that silence I saw Gail fishing a riffle upstream of what was then the Henderson tannery,

With a pained expression on his face, Sam shifted in his seat. "With all your doubts, it must be wrenching to write."

"Yes. One self scratching sentences on notepaper awakens a second self making arguments against what is being written down. The two threads of thought run concurrently. Nothing I can say will capture the whole truth. I write because writing is something I must do to earn an income. Penury mutes my inner doubts. There is hardly a sentence of my writing I do not personally dispute, but if I waited to form a perfectly truthful expression of what I am trying to say, I would never finish a paragraph. It is the same with my fishing. Every cast brings doubt. My only relief comes from thinking of fly fishing as a lifelong experiment without hope of a final epiphany. This last thought is probably as close as I can get to the truth."

"You have argued that fishing is a harmless enjoyment. Now you are making it sound like drudgery." Mrs. Henderson said pointedly.

"For others it is a distraction which they can pursue if they so feel. I have no choice. For me fly fishing is what life demands of me. It is my portion."

"It's getting late. Mrs. Henderson took down your advice last time you were here. It was very helpful." Briefly Sam stared hard at his wife to quiet her. "Do you have another piece of advice for me tonight?" Sam asked.

I looked over to see a smirking Mrs. Henderson, then turning back said to Sam, "Yes. Fish the glare."

"I don't understand," Sam said.

"Another of your vague *nostrums*, Mr. Gordon?" Asked Mrs. Henderson.

"No. Just common sense. Trout are naturally skittish. Most of their enemies strike from above so they flee whenever a shadow falls over them. Don't allow your shadow to fall on the river."

"Easier said than done Mr. Gordon." Mrs. Henderson shot back.

"Before you cast always check the sun. You want it opposite you so the fish are between you and the sun. This is always my first concern when I take up a position to cast. It may mean longer walks and challenging wading, but it gives you the advantage. If your shadow falls on a fish, nothing you do can make up for it.

Remember if you can see the fish, they can see you. The glare shields you from them and them from you."

Mrs. Henderson opened her mouth to speak but I interrupted anticipating her question. "Surely Lady Campbell mentioned this to you?"

"Yes. But on the Neversink it's difficult advice to follow."

"True, but the Neversink flows generally north to south so you should have little difficulty finding your shadow. Mornings the sun will shine from the East so hug the west bank. Vice versa in the afternoon. Of course, the best days are the ones of dark overcast with the clouds hovering just above your head. A dark lowering day as one savant called it. A day for dun colored flies. A day like today."

"Thank you Mr. Gordon," Sam said. Mrs. Henderson was silent. I tried to understand her reticence, then added, "Of course if you can't maneuver the glare between yourself and the fish, then just fish the glare. You'd be surprised how often you catch something." That was certainly enough value for my meal. I anticipated more fly orders from Sam.

After dessert, Mrs. Henderson hurried the evening to a close. "Ann, have you made up Mr. Gordon's room?"

"Yes, Ma'am."

"I wish to thank you for your fish tonight and your conversation. It was most...illuminating...so unlike you. I must order Mr. Lanier's poems."

"They are worth your effort."

Later at the door to my room, Ann said "My father recited poetry at our dinner table. Your words brought back happier times with my family. Thank you. You are like no other person who dines with us."

Before leaving Ann asked, "Is there anything I can get for you?"

"If you wouldn't mind, a glass of milk punch."

"Never heard of it, Mr. Gordon."

"It's a drink I enjoyed mornings in Savannah. Half a glass of milk, a little cream would help, two shots of brandy or whisky, I prefer brandy, a little sugar and nutmeg sprinkled on top."

"Egg nog without the egg. Give me a minute." When she returned, I was coughing. "You worry me Mr. Gordon," she said placing the glass of punch on top of the chest of drawers. "You sound like my father towards the end. He died of consumption as did so many of us on the lower east side."

"You were spared."

"Through the intercession of St. Eulalia, my Lady of the Camellias."

"Superstition!"

"Few of us can afford being as skeptical as you," Ann murmured, frowning.

"Please forgive me. Long ago I gave up asking for help from the next world. It never arrived."

"I'll keep you in my prayers," she smiled and turned to leave, "I need my rest." A few steps toward the door, she turned again inhaling deeply, "Don't you love the air up here?"

I smiled, took a sip of milk punch, and journeyed back to Savannah. Its milliners, the City Market and the Habershams.

# 6

## Savannah and the Habershams

Savannah's warm climate coddled me. It was so different from this hard mountain country. At the end of the Civil War, my Mother, Fanny Gordon, left Pittsburgh, where I was born, and traveled the South with me in tow. We tarried a few years in Mobile where she was raised and where my father died of malaria. After Mobile there were other stops. We never stayed long in any of them. Finally, Mother and I moved to Savannah, where the Gordon name is common. Our relatives fussed over her, and she proved herself an engaging conversationalist albeit a chronic invalid by then. She spent her energies searching for a wife for me.

In Savannah the Civil War's austerities hung on long after Sherman left. Unlike Atlanta, it showed no scars, and so had no public explanation for its poverty. Savannah's loyalty had always been to itself. In the decades following its capitulation to the Army of the West, it became a widow living in reduced circumstances, servants dismissed, rooms closed up, dust covers everywhere. One day a Confederate flag flew from her porch, the next, the stars and stripes snapped smartly in the sea breeze. The switch no more noteworthy than a change of bedding on wash day.

Thus when Mother and I took up residence, Savannah stood strangely outsized for its purposes. It was a city striving to live up to its past like a child puffing itself up to fill out hand-me-downs from older siblings. Nostalgia panhandled on every street corner. Poorly tended squares, reminders of what had been, became the charge of neighborhood women stretching their time, their servants' time, and their budgets, planting fresh flowers and ornamental trees. Over the years, they planted more and more perennials and pulled fewer and fewer weeds. Clubs put on lavish shows reminiscent of pre-war galas only to disband when the membership could not cover the bills. So many frame houses went unpainted. From street to street, the hodgepodge of repairs bespoke the idiosyncrasies and reduced circumstances of their owners. Outer neighborhoods declined. And the city, a port city, grew a coarse underbelly. Visitors began to call it seedy.

Mother and I enjoyed it. We lived on stock investments, principally the Central of Georgia Railroad. Without fail it paid annual dividends, eight percent on average. Flush with income, we rented rooms on President Street facing Oglethorpe Square. Listing myself as a broker of stocks and bonds, I rented an office on Drayton Street, just off Factor's Walk, and joined the yacht club.

Savannah lived outdoors, reveling in the seasons, the rise and fall of the tides, the onrush of storms off the Atlantic, and the migration of birds up and down the coast. With less wealth came more leisure. More lawn parties, more Sunday visiting, more casual conversations. Business was done over long lunches. And our money went farther. We hired a cook who fed us grits and shrimp for breakfast, a wartime austerity the city retained long after the war ended. On mornings when my breathing labored, our maid put out milk punch for me. Fishing and hunting were acceptable excuses for taking time off work. Success meant one less trip to the City Market for an entrée. A penny saved.

Another sip of milk punch, and I was in our apartment on Oglethorp Square. It was afternoon. A note from the Habershams had just arrived by messenger. An invitation for me to visit them at Avon, their country home over the weekend. Fishing and then a small family dinner with their grandchildren, Mary and George Noble. I read the invitation aloud to Mother.

Elated, she interpreted the message for me, "This invitation means they're considering you as a match for Mary. Your light summer suit is appropriate."

"So I believe,"

"No one's caught Mary's eye?"

"The word at the Yacht Club is she's too particular."

"That's hardly a fault. She would make a great catch."

"Her intelligence frightens men off."

"You're her equal."

"Hardly, Mother. She will benefit from the Habersham fortune."

"Theodore, I'm just saying engage her in serious conversation. Listen to her! My greatest disappointment is that we have not found you a wife."

"It's not that you haven't tried, Mother."

"I don't mean to be critical but sometimes around women you can be forbiddingly aloof. When you make the effort, you can be very entertaining." She paused and then charged ahead, "Charm her! You two would make the perfect couple. She'll have the money, and you can manage it."

"It's not a matter of money, Mother. It's a matter of real estate. We've never had any."

Shaking a finger at me, her eyes flashed, "Remember you're a respected businessman."

"Mother, you overstate my position. It's just me, a desk and a few Wall Street connections.

"Charm her...please" Her voice sounded piteous, "For my sake Theodore."

I relented, "I'll do my best, Mother."

"Indulge me. It would make me so happy to see you married."

"I know," I said smiling.

"And spend less time with that grandfather of hers trading fish stories."

"I like the whole family," I said apologetically.

And then it was Saturday, and I was on the White Bluff Road, my horse's hooves thudding on its bed of crushed oyster shells. Skirting the ocean, the road ran through a tunnel of live oak hung with Spanish moss. It was summer, the time of straw hats and billowy cotton dresses. Fashionable young men and women stood together silhouetted on wood-planked docks talking, looking out to sea. Parasoled mothers walked hand in hand with their children along the shore. Beneath the sharp smell of sea air hung the sluggish scent of salt marsh, the odor of decay and promise. With the tide in, more promise than decay. With the tide out and the mud flats exposed more decay than promise.

After the War Neyle Habersham and his wife Josephine took up living at Avon Hall. Until then it had been the family summer place. When Sherman occupied Savannah, Neyle, a prominent Confederate supporter, thought it best to vacate the city and so escape daily scrutiny. He kept a business office and warehouse on Bay Street which his son Robert managed.

Arriving early to catch the tide, I left my horse with a stable boy. Bait casting rod, Kentucky reel, and gunny sack in hand, I crossed the lawn to the Vernon River. A servant handed me a note. "Possum Island and Coffee Bluff," Neyle's instructions for where to find channel bass, our dinner. I waived my "yes" back to the Hall. Neyle's white head bobbed at his study window.

Near Avon, the Vernon is narrow. Pushing a rowboat downriver, my squeaking oars startled white ibis. They rose, wheeled overhead, and winged downriver skimming rust colored cord grass and green reed stands. So much loosed cotton adrift in the breeze. The little boat caught a leisurely current, and I cast a spinner trailed by a Scarlet Ibis into every opening in the reeds. A few small bass fell for it, too small for the kitchen. Then I put my rod down and pulled hard for Possum Island and the Ogeechee. As the river broadened and grew more sluggish, I added buckshot and lengthened my casts. The fish were bigger, their runs longer, and I lost a few at the boat having forgotten a net.

A few more sips of Ann's milk punch. The Vernon swells, and the tide turns, pushing me back upriver. My gunny sack full of keepers, I rowed rhythmically for the hall. Overhead, an eagle patrolled for what the sea threw up, and I watched it glide silently high up. And high up I heard the notes of Neyle's flute. A Mozart piece piping the angler home. The notes full and powerful, it is a marvel that at eighty he still had the breath.

Between bites at dinner, I reported, "Never made it to Coffee Bluff. Caught more bass than needed off Possum Island. I kept only the best size for eating." Neyle was pleased. Mary and her brother George Noble, however, sat silent, intent on the full plates before them. Scaled and gutted, the bass were baked whole and served on a bed of saffron rice their juices dripping.

"I don't like the skin," Mary said making a face. "I've never liked the skin. It tastes mucky."

"Sweet one, it tastes of the marsh," Josephine cooed. "We owe so much to the marshes." Turning her head she then whispered to Mary, 'I do not believe "mucky" is a word for a proper young lady.'

Neyle chuckled. "Let's find a better word. How about silty? That has a smooth sound, slippery like a fish."

"What do you think Mr. Gordon?" Mary asked.

"It tastes substantial, healthy," I said winking at Mary before taking another bite with the skin on. "But of course I'm prejudiced. These bass accepted my invitation to dinner."

"Next time, Mary darling, we'll dredge them in flour and crushed mint. A few drops of lime should take the edge off the marsh taste," Josephine said looking over with a smile.

"The Reynolds stuff them with crab and cayenne sauce, then coat them with mayonnaise, Grandmother."

"They'll lose the flavor of the marsh altogether. That's too great a price to pay."

Neyle asked, "George Noble what do you think?"

"I praise whatever is put in front of me, sir."

"So young and so adroit. Are we raising a politician?"

As Mother wished, I engaged Mary raising subjects I guessed to her liking and listening encouragingly when she spoke. Several times she smiled at me when I took up her thoughts. And each time, in retreat, she quickly glanced over at her grandmother.

Finally towards the end of dinner, Josephine announced, "Mr. Gordon, we're serving a special dessert in your honor tonight. A Gordon family recipe."

"I cannot imagine what that might be. My mother and I are creatures of boarding houses and hotels."

"Your family here calls it Apple Betty. A very simple recipe, diced sour apples, bread crumbs, brown sugar, cinnamon, and butter baked in layers. We will have it tonight with a vanilla cream sauce."

When dessert was finished, I thanked Josephine. "I'm overwhelmed with your thoughtfulness. You've taught me something new about the Gordons."

"I'm saving a serving dish full for your mother."

"You are too gracious."

With that Josephine looked sharply at Neyle prodding him with her silence until he roused himself. "Theodore, let us retire to my study for a glass of Madeira." I began to rise from my chair when George Noble pleaded, "Grandfather couldn't I join you? I'm old enough to drink wine."

Neyle looked over to Josephine who sat silent, distant, "Your grandmother puts on the face of *La Giaconda*, George Noble. I'm guessing she agrees with you. So with her tacit approval, I say it is time for you to learn the secrets of Madeira."

"Thank you, Grandfather."

Mary glanced up at me and frowned. To her grandmother she said, "I'm older than George Noble."

Josephine was unmoved. "Let the men go, Mary dear. Ours will be the greater enjoyment. We will sip sherry and become insightful."

"Mrs. Habersham, will you give us men a clue of what is better than our company?"

"No, Theodore. Remember you're not leaving us women behind. We're shooing you away."

Neyle laughed, "Ever so."

On the way to Neyle's study, left alone with my own thoughts, I concluded I would soon be out of the running for Mary's hand. No property, little wealth, and the probability of building a fortune without capital unlikely. I had neither the magnetic personality nor the unbounded energy needed for such an endeavor. And then there were my bouts with consumption. All this was obvious to Josephine and she would make it obvious to Mary by the end of their evening chat. It was true I had displayed wit, was well informed, and showed Mary deference, yet these would not be enough. Many young men in Savannah could match my performance and many of them many enjoyed comfortable wealth.

In a corner of Neyle's study, a room of tall louvered shutters, a half dozen dusty bottles and crystal port glasses crowded a marquetry credenza. We sat in black Windsor chairs. Neyle filled two glasses full and a third, half-full. He handed George Noble the half-full glass. "Madeira is fortified with brandy so it has more alcohol than wine. I want you alert for your first experience of it."

"Sir, some criticize you for storing Madeira pipes on the upper floors of Bay Street. Especially during the hot summers?" George Noble put it as a query. I had heard the same criticisms.

"Madeira needs tropical heat to mature. The hotter the better. That is one of its secrets." Neyle explained and then looked sharply at his grandson, "You will not repeat that. To be profitable, every business must have its secrets."

"Of course, sir."

"Some of my Bay Street pipes your grandchildren will enjoy years from now. The bottle we're now enjoying was drawn from a pipe of malmsey put up before the War. It is one of my special blends. Another secret."

"Theodore you possess an acute sense of color. How would you describe for George Noble the colors in your glass?

The sun sat arrested on the horizon sending long scarlet rays across the lawn. Holding up the glass, I swirled the liquid and let it settle. "The evening light has a scarlet cast, so I will deduct that from the color of the Madeira. I see generally a tawny color with amber edges. When disturbed it flashes orange and purple. That is the best I can do, sir, in this light."

"Very perceptive, Theodore. George Noble, you will always find those colors in good malmsey Madeira."

"Yes, sir." He sipped.

"How does it taste?"

"Sweet."

"Anything else."

"A taste of molasses followed by a slight bitterness."

"Madeira has many flavors, and each time you drink it you must identify them, and commit them to memory. Tonight the sweetness is there with the molasses taste followed by the bitterness. Well done. You will discover more in days to come."

Neyle shifted in his chair, "Theodore, I was happy to read your recent piece in the *Fishing Gazette*. The British appreciate your writing."

"I needed to remind them that Thad Norris recommended fishing dry flies fifteen years before the British author Frederic Halford touted them in his *Floating Flies*. Maybe I was a trifle nationalistic but the editor, Mr. Marston, didn't seem to mind. I correspond regularly with him."

Neyle turned to George Noble, "Norris is a Philadelphian. You will find his book very helpful even for fishing here in Savannah. A universal mind. You can borrow my copy." As an afterthought, he said, "Dry flies are flies tied to sit on top of the water." George Noble nodded, and Neyle turned back to me, "Have you mentioned to Marston that I caught salmon on the Restigouche using dry flies."

"Yes. He was surprised but unconvinced. His main interest is fishing dry flies to chalk stream brown trout. A very different proposition from fishing Canadian rivers like the Restigouche."

Neyle chuckled, "I've been told that Halford would have us fishing dry flies for flounder."

"I will say in his favor that he is a very generous man. I was quite taken with his most recent work, *Dry Fly Entomology* and wrote him a lengthy letter praising the book. He sent me a full set of his dry flies in appreciation. Next summer I'll test them in the Catskills."

"Did you bring the salmon flies you promised, Theodore?"

"Yes, two Silver Doctors, one wet and one dry." I reached in my pocket for a small box and placed it next to his glass. "My gift to you."

Neyle pulled a battered fly wallet from a desk drawer. Leafing through it, he said, "There should be at least one Silver Doctor here, a wet." He found it and carefully teased it out. "Hardy's sent me this one," he said holding the fly up to catch the lamplight. It flashed silver and blue. Holding up one of my flies side by side with the Hardy, he said, "Theodore, you tie as well as Hardy's best."

George Noble stood up to look. "Hardy?"

"England's finest tackle maker." Neyle smiled at his grandson.

"They're beautiful. How long does it take to tie one?"

"For these, three hours. I'd some trouble finding silver tinsel that would lie flat. The hook is from Hardy's and the feathers and tinsel from Savannah's millinery shops."

We talked on. Neyle's voice dispelled clocks and schedules, invoking a timeless space into which we dropped words. Every story he told unhurriedly to its end, without interruption. And just when I thought a story was exhausted and was ready to propose a new subject, Neyle opened a new prospect in what we were discussing. Throughout I fought the urge to hurry his pace. Once, sensing my impatience, he looked over and said, "We must fully ventilate what we perceive."

"Sorry, sir; my tendency is to jump from one subject to another and then to circle back again opening and closing each subject again and again. You stay with one until it's exhausted."

"I have my method, you have yours. Both have their virtues. You spend your time striking one subject against another looking to spark something new. My preference is less heat."

We were reaching the bottom of the Madeira bottle when Neyle brought up his last salmon fishing trip to the Restigouche River. "I have not yet recovered."

He studied his glass of Madeira twirling the stem, "I was impatient. My Canadian hosts telegraphed suggesting I delay my trip to wait for milder weather. Believing they were patronizing me on account of my age, I set out early to prove them wrong. Wanting to be the first on the river, I made the trip a few weeks after ice out. I fished from a leaky canoe in cold rains and high winds. My feet were always wet, and I ignored my Mi'kmaq guides when they advised me to return to shore and warm up every few hours. Instead I stayed out whole days with indifferent results. One salmon, twenty-five pounds."

"Young men are allowed to be foolish." He took a sip. "A failure in judgment," he said slowly and with great feeling. "Impatience is expected in the young. It is inexcusable in a man of eighty. I am mending…slowly." He paused, "I'll go one more spring and, after that, will sell my beat."

Next morning Mary appeared alone in the stable yard to say "Good-bye." I read pity in her eyes. While we men were drinking Madeira, she discussed me with her grandmother. A consumptive possessed of little property. Any woman marrying me need be wealthy and inclined to nursing if she hoped to stay in society and grow old with me. Mary was cultivated, beautiful and kind, worth any man's suit. So too she was innocent, bred for the protected life in which she was raised. So I retreated, and she, grateful, sensed it. She knew, as I, that challenging the implacable rules of polite Savannah society and the inevitable progression of my disease was futile.

From horseback, wheeling about, I blew her a kiss and with a theatrical bow and a downward sweep of my straw hat, I said a heartfelt, "'Til we meet again, milady." Flirting is always acceptable in Savannah. Mary smiled, and I will remember that smile until that day my lungs drown in phlegm. It did not matter that pity underlay her concern. Her unrestrained smile lifted me up. In future days, I would never be more than a guest in her house, but I knew I would be an honored guest. And that would be enough. Small shows of love sustained me in Savannah where wealthy young women knew their worth.

Riding back to Oglethorpe Square, I wondered if I would make forty.

I did. So tonight, warm, I drowse with the taste of milk punch on my tongue. And looking into the dark, I see Mary as she was that Savannah morning. And I think on Opening Day.

# 7

## Bread Board

One day or was it night, Jeanie lent me an old bread board. And she added another pillow to my bed so I could sit up. Balancing the board on my knees, I write letters longhand or type fishing articles with my little Underwood. On my low days, not much else is left me. Lonely, always lonely, I reach out. Last night, I typed two short articles, one for *The Fishing Gazette* and the other for *Forest and Stream*. The companionship they bring will be short lived, two small checks and a few earnest comments, perhaps laudatory.

Loneliness tempts me to controversy. Pick a side and find a loyal, outspoken constituency, long lived allies demanding no more of an author than a clear, antagonistic position and stubbornness. Presently all of Europe is at war, and we in the United States are debating whether to join in. Claiming patriotism, sports magazines open their pages to this debate. I am against the United States entering the war and am disgusted that our sports magazines encourage furious debate when they should be reporting on fishing and hunting.

The *Gazette* article discusses the merits of American Meadow Lark feathers for fly tying. A Savannah correspondent sent me a whole skin. The yellow breast feathers will supply soft hackle for yellow legged flies. The note is short and to ensure its publication, I will mail it with the skin, a personal gift to Marston.

The second article goes to *Forest and Stream*. It is about leaders, a subject I have addressed often enough. So I am glib. My assignment was to test gut leaders dyed to match the colors of different waters. Dr. Breck, an accomplished chemist and an enthusiastic angler, did the dyeing. I have a rough and ready method for camouflaging leaders which I have never shared with the public. Thus I made no test of Dr. Breck's leaders. What the editors will receive instead is a long piece, short on information, and no help for the ignorant. My own method is quite simple. Make certain the leader sinks. Avoid touching it with any grease on your fingers and soak it for hours in a leader box. If necessary, I scour my leaders with river sand.

Only letter writing dispels my loneliness. Never too tired to feel lonely, I am never too tired to scratch out a letter. Calling the recipient's name to mind, my pen delivers their company. The closing and my signature affixed, the scratching stops, and the recipient departs. Loneliness returns, and I lay back coughing. Staring into my bedside lamp, I wait for a new name to form in the lamp's chimney. It does and shortly my pen delivers companionship with the warm salutation. Lately, no longer trusting my correspondents' sympathy, I admit my loneliness and plead for a reply.

No matter how lonely, some names appearing in my lamp's chimney do not tempt me to write. One is Halford. My correspondence with him ended sourly years ago. Without explanation he just stopped replying to my letters and gifts. An intended slight, for certain, so after a few more unanswered inquiries, I decided to end my correspondence him and have never revisited my decision. It became irrevocable last year when he died.

All my customers are amateurs. A few have caught onto the fact that I have little money. But they have not caught on to how much of that little comes from fly tying. They think me a romantic figure, a mendicant, vowed to meditate on the mysteries of trout fishing, thoughtless of my own needs, impoverished by my many pilgrimages made on their behalf. To mask my commercial ends, I become what they want, a selfless elder, a chatty friend, an honored initiate in the Brotherhood of the Angle. They see my flies as reports from a better world and the accompanying invoices as reminders to reimburse my costs.

My wealthy customers spread this rosy gloss among their kind. New customers come to me by word of mouth from other worthies who vouch for my flies as being "right on the money." They endow fly fishing with an otherworldly purity and appoint me the keeper of the flame. Polite, informative replies keep them in my circle. Their orders for flies come in the course of cordial, leisured correspondence, never from a catalog or newspaper advertisement. They look forward to my letters, for my letters give them respite from their desperate world of balance sheets and rampant greed. I advise each personally, custom work from the hands of their priest, their dedicated friend in the country, the sort of products Habersham counseled me to manufacture, products bespeaking an ideal world, all within my ken and my ken alone. The guise works well but not well enough. The Brotherhood supports me by buying my flies, but they never pay enough for me to put money aside.

Today in the mail I received a letter from Guy Jenkins. He ordered dozens of flies. I need set aside a few weeks to fill his order. My strength is now at low ebb. It will take several days just to tie a few dozen Coachmen, a favorite pattern of his. I will do them in bed tying by hand.

# 8

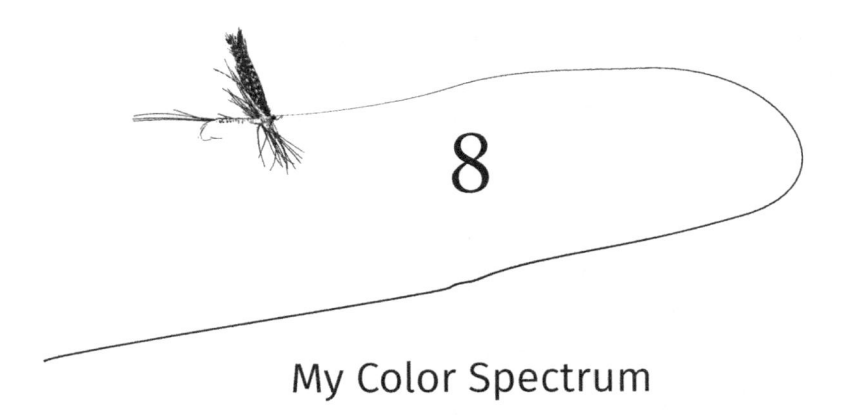

## My Color Spectrum

My deepest convictions about fly fishing for trout formed slowly. Fishless days and the gnawing confusion born of failure were my first teachers. Reading, observation, and experimentation followed. All seemed hit and miss until the testimony of my eyes, the hundreds of humble observations made out fishing, knit together to form a fundamental conviction. This conviction rests on the firmest of foundations, namely, fishing, years of fishing. I have spent more time fly fishing for trout than anyone I know, certainly more than any writer I know.

A single, succinct sentence captures the gist of what I know about catching trout with flies. To succeed, the angler must put the right color fly in front of the trout. Color precedes all other considerations, including size and profile. The right color fly catches fish. The wrong color fly does not.

Trout are not picky eaters. They must feed to survive and so will strike any fly the color of the food they are eating. The food they eat are mayflies, caddis flies, stoneflies, craneflies, beetles, ants, etc. and the colors of such foods are black, dun, gray/brown, light brown, tan, tan/green, green, brown/gold, gold, pale yellow, and finally cream. These colors fall on a spectrum I have worked out over years of fishing. My favorite flies matching the colors of my spectrum are: the Black Gnat and Grannom for black, the Quill

Gordon for dun, the Dark Cahill for brown/gray, the Mink Fly for light brown, the Gold Ribbed Hare's Ear for tan, the "Good Dun" for tan/green, the Blue Winged Olive for green, the Gordon for gold, the Pale Evening Dun for pale yellow, and the Light Cahill for the lightest tan and cream.

Some of the flies matching the colors on my spectrum, I tie in shades. My Pale Evening Dun is tied in four shades. My Quill, the Larva, the Dark Cahill, and the Light Cahill I tie in three shades each, light, medium, and dark. The Gold Ribbed Hare's Ear, the "Good Dun," and the Gordon are tied in two shades, light and dark. My remaining favorite flies—the Black Gnat, the Grannom, the Mink Fly, the Beetle, and the Crane Fly—are tied in a single shade. The Mink Fly and the Crane Fly are tied in a beige/tan. The others, all black flies, are tied in a pitch black.

Finding the right color is not the end of the matter. To be successful, an angler must put the right colored fly before the trout. It is no great leap of logic to identify the places where trout feed. The options are limited: either above the surface of the water, in the surface film, or below the surface of the water. Such differences can be measured in fractions of inches. In the last stages of their short life, aquatic insects spend their time contending with the river's surface. The healthy mayfly dun floats on the river's surface and then flies off to transform into a spinner and mate. Healthy duns are true dry flies. The crippled dun unable to free itself from its nymphal shuck, the emerging dun doused by spray, the spent spinner alighting onto the river in its death throes, and the wind-blown beetle and ant, all become mired in the surface film. Finally, drowned cripples, spinners, and waterlogged terrestrials sink below the river's surface and tumble along beneath the surface of the river.

The right colored fly appearing at the right spot in the water column I call "the effective fly." This is the fly successful anglers fish. I came to this realization by accident. Among the many fishing books I read are Frederic Halford's books promoting dry fly fishing. His writings filled me with fervor for the dry fly method. Catskill trout cooled that ardor. In the period when I began to question dry fly fishing, I fished a cast of two flies, a high floating dry fly of Halford's design and a wet fly of my own design. One day sitting by a run, I saw three trout rising upstream. No time to lose, I false cast both flies while wading into position. Both flies dried and both flies floated. One after another, all three rising trout struck and were hooked, but not to Halford's high floating dry. Rather, they struck my sparsely tied, low floating wet fly. The lesson was obvious. I should trust my own sparsely tied flies, flies that could double both as a low floating dry fly or a wet fly.

Building on this experience, I now carry both full ties and sparse ties. The full are tied with two hackles; the sparse are tied with a single hackle. The hackles I use are hardly as long as my little finger, four or five turns about the shaft of the hook at most. The two hackle flies ride above the surface. My single hackle flies barely float in the surface film and will on occasion sink beneath it, thus imitating drowned naturals slipping under the water's surface.

For Halford, La Branche, and all scientific anglers, there are only dry flies. For Skues, there are wet and dry flies. For me, there is a third fly—my sparse tie—that roams the border between wet and dry.

The notion of tying dry flies that sink runs contrary to the preaching of scientific angling. Halford and his followers in this country, La Branche and Emlyn Gill, demand their dry flies float without exception. If their dry flies sink, fishing necessarily ends because, as Halford says, fishing becomes unscientific and so unethical. When tying for scientific anglers, my wealthier clients, I give them what they want, namely, double hackled, high floating unsinkable dries.

For a commercial tier to produce a dry fly that sinks is shameful. This prospect does not stop me when tying flies for myself. I am not a scientific angler, but a practitioner of what I call "rough and ready" fly fishing. The sparse fly is my most closely held secret, and its disclosure would threaten to out me as a heretic to the true faith of scientific angling. Such publicity would destroy my business.

Only local friends like Bruce LeRoy, Roy Steenrod, and Herman Christian, and my faithful British correspondent, Skues, know of my invention. The uninitiated glancing through my fly boxes have not caught on to my system. So many of my flies are traditional patterns, some tied sparse and some, full, all in different shades. Those insensitive to shades of color, as most anglers are, hardly notice the differences.

The angler finds the "effective fly" by "ringing the colors." This strategy is simple to explain. I go through my color spectrum, fishing above, flush in, or below the stream's surface until I start getting strikes. To facilitate the constant changing among colors, I carry snelled flies. Evening is my favorite time to fish. With my poor eyesight, the dying light makes threading a tippet through a hook's eye impossible. Snelled flies make the switch easy to accomplish, nothing more than unlooping one fly and looping on another. Regarding snelled flies, I, with Skues, believe some fly patterns are more effectively fished snelled.

At the beginning of every day, the first question the fly fisher asks is, "What fly do I put on?" Or as I ask myself, "What is the effective fly today?" The search must begin with the realization that this day of fishing will be like no other. The fly fisher must revel in what makes this day unique. Listen to what the river tells you, then make a guess, remembering always your guess is tentative. Yes, cast your fly with confidence, but keep doubting you are casting the effective fly.

Halford and his scientific anglers select the fly that matches the natural on the water. It is always a dry fly. Halford gives microscopic descriptions of floating insects. Once the insect is identified, he provides the name and dressing of the matching artificial fly. One snag, however. If trout are not rising, the scientific angler need wait until they do. A second snag follows close on. If trout are rising to naturals and Halford's recommended imitation does not attract strikes, the angler confronts a harder problem: "What fly do I put on next?" No longer able to rely on the theory of matching the natural, the scientific angler must improvise. In this event,

Halford prescribes a sequence of flies to follow up, depending on the situation. Again, all are high floating dry flies. But what is the angler to do when this sequence of flies does not attract a rise? And very often it does not because trout may be rising to naturals in or underneath the surface. In that situation, the scientific angler must wait for the appearance of a high floating natural that can be imitated.

The strength of ringing the colors is that it expects failure. The overwhelming likelihood is that no one cast will produce a strike. Failure is endemic to fly fishing. If neither the first, nor the second, nor the third fly succeed, ringing the colors will give the angler more choices above, in, or below the surface, as needed. Sooner or later, by a process of elimination, ringing the colors will put the angler onto the effective fly. That has been my experience.

Scientific anglers have go-to-flies. For Halford, it was the Gold Ribbed Hare's Ear and the Red Quill. For La Branche, it is the Whirling Blue Dun and the Pink Lady. I do not have a go-to fly. I have a go-to method, namely, ringing the colors. I discipline myself not to become emotionally attached to any one fly. Most of my favorite flies, most days, do not produce. But all I need is one or two that do, and these I find by ringing the colors.

It is worth keeping in mind that ringing the color demands discipline. Some mornings, my energy exhausted, my condition more so of late, I hesitate going out. When no trout rise to my first fly, I repeat to myself, "Change colors; change colors." With a sheer act of will, I do change flies. A tedious task, a task requiring attention. The old fly slipped off and stowed in its proper place, a shuffling among boxes, a new color fly selected and carefully threaded on the tippet, a testing of the knot, the knot failing and the fly rethreaded and reknotted. With all the fly changing, some flies drop into the river, and some are filed away in the wrong compartment of the wrong box. In the end, I whisper, "Get ahold of yourself. Change flies! Ring the colors." And sure enough most days ringing the colors produces fish.

In the Beaverkill below the Covered Bridge is a stretch that holds two pools, as many rapids, and a long curving run. The river varies between forty and fifty feet across.

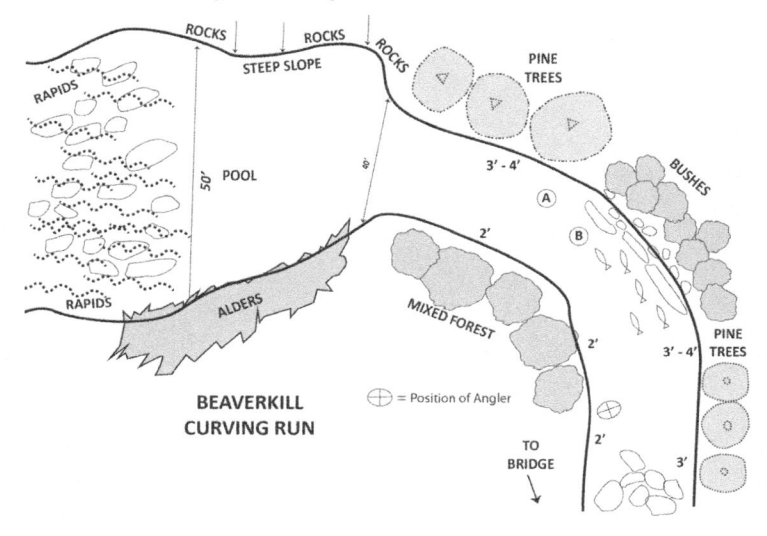

[Diagram: map of Beaverkill Curving Run showing rapids, 50' pool, steep slope, rocks, pine trees, bushes, mixed forest, alders, with positions of angler marked at points A and B, depths of 2', 3'-4', and an arrow pointing "TO BRIDGE"]

One evening in the early days of becoming proficient with ringing the colors, I tried my sparse hackled Quill on the swift, curving run. Having rung the colors first with several shades of the Cahill and the light and dark Gold Ribbed Hare's Ear, all high floaters, without result, I put on a size twelve sparse version of my Quill and cast to Point A. The fly sat in the film, floated a few yards, and due to the turbulence, sank as sparsely tied flies tend to do in rough water. At Point B, it slipped below the surface, still dead drift, and was immediately attacked by two trout: a brook and a brown. The larger fish, the brown won, and was creeled. Snapping the moisture off my Quill, I cast upstream again, and once again at the instant the fly sank, it was taken by the brook.

Two weeks later, still mulling the curving run experience, I was fishing a small pool on the Willowemoc, the far side deeper by a few feet than the one from which I was casting.

Eight trout were working in the deeper water across from me, a few occasionally rising. No naturals were in evidence. Putting on a size sixteen sparsely tied, single winged light Quill, I cast

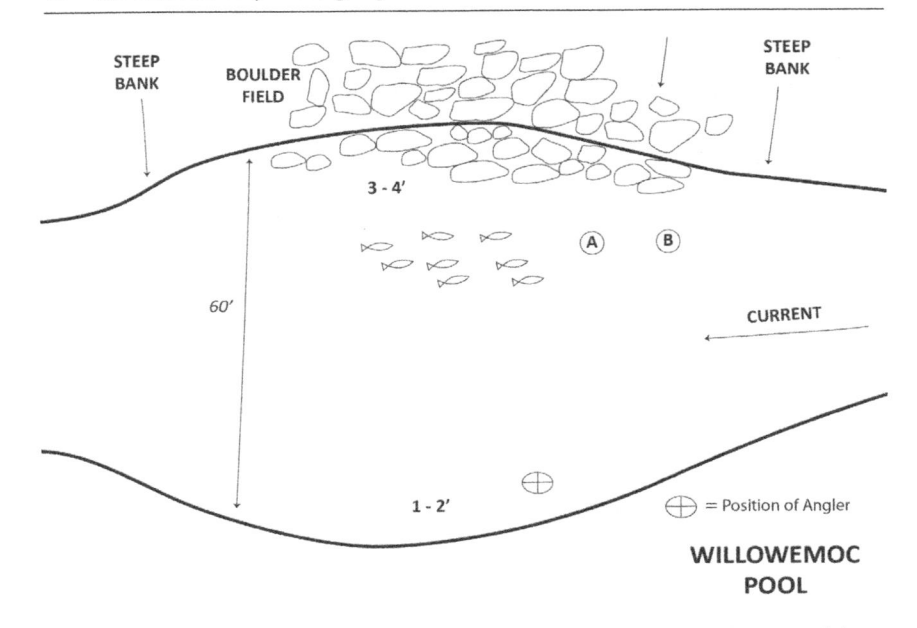

```
STEEP                              STEEP
BANK    BOULDER                    BANK
        FIELD

                3 - 4'

                          (A)  (B)

        60'                              CURRENT


                   1 - 2'  ⊕
                                    ⊕ = Position of Angler

                              WILLOWEMOC
                              POOL
```

to Point A and caught a few risers on the surface, but then nothing. Luckily, the remaining fish continued feeding, apparently not spooked by my casts. Remembering the curving run experience, I cast to Point B and then twitched my Quill, sinking it. Drifting just under the surface, my Quill took five more. My conclusion, color is all important, but where in the water column the angler shows that color is just as important. This day, it seemed a few trout were looking for the right colored fly on the surface while the rest were looking for the same colored fly underneath the surface. By showing the color in both places, success was assured.

A few miles downstream from the Beaverkill Covered Bridge, the river washes up against a steep embankment. The river gradient is severe and the river picks up speed, rushing headlong into it. It then bends east at a right angle and becomes almost two distinct streams running together shoulder to shoulder. The stream running alongside the embankment is deeper and faster with many boulders and a few deadfalls caught up along the bank. The other stream, running along the north side of the river, is shallower with a slower flow.

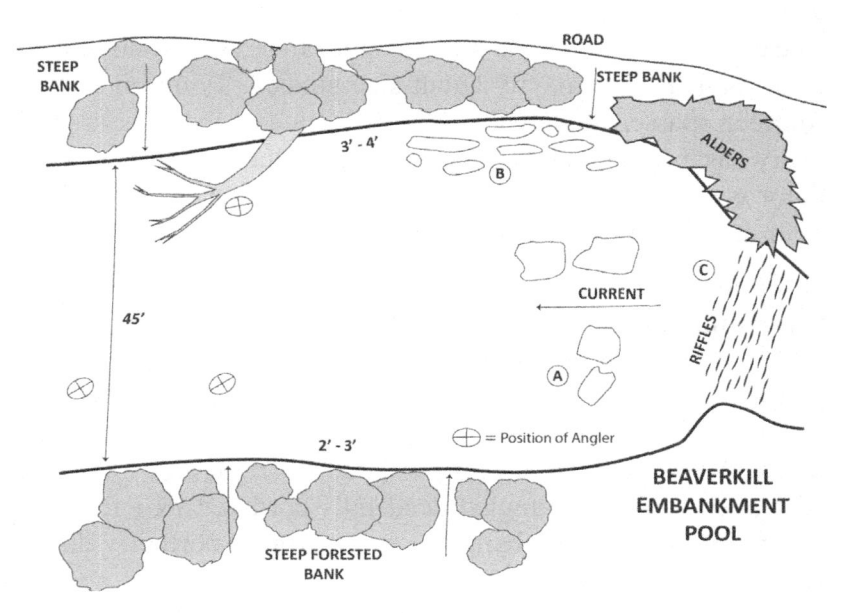

*Theodore Gordon: His Lost Flies and Last Sentiments ~ 67*

[Diagram of BEAVERKILL EMBANKMENT POOL showing: ROAD at top, STEEP BANK on upper left and upper right, ALDERS on right, RIFFLES on right side, CURRENT arrow pointing left, STEEP FORESTED BANK at bottom. Depths marked "3'-4'" and "2'-3'", width "45'". Points A, B, C marked. Symbol ⊕ = Position of Angler.]

    Because this pool is of two minds, the angler's approach must address both. Ringing the colors must be done separately for each side. One July mid-day, on the slow side, casting to Point A, I rang the colors from Pale Evening Dun, to light and dark Gold Ribbed Hare's Ear, and then the dark Dark Cahill. None produced a rise. A size fourteen dark version of my Quill was next, and it connected with three fish, all brook trout. Shifting to the fast side, I again rang the colors, a dark Dark Cahill initially brought a few tentative rises, then nothing. Wading up a few yards, I changed to a number twelve light Gordon. Casting to Point B, eleven casts brought nine strikes and five decent fish, brook and brown. Then a lull, so shifting back to the slower side with the Gordon, I came up empty until, changing to a sparse, single wing, number sixteen dark Quill, I caught five more.

    Mid-day a week later in the same pool, a number twelve medium Dark Cahill moved a few fish; then the river went dead. Wading upstream, I rang the colors both sides, the Gordon, two shades of sparse Dark Cahills, a Light Cahill, and the Mink Fly. Nothing. All the while, I was wondering, "Where are the fish?" The answer was that they were feeding at the very head of the pool: Point C. The trout had moved up to intercept the emergers and floating duns of a grayish olive mayfly about size sixteen. Tying on a number fourteen sparse, single wing, light Quill, I cast for an hour. Nearly every cast brought a fish. The size of my Quill was wrong, but the color was right, and it looked right on the river. For this fleeting hour, it was, without doubt, the effective fly.

On another day, the last week of August, a few years later, I was fishing the Esopus below Phoenicia. It was a stretch of water with a sharply dropping gradient. A vigorous rapids, seventy-five feet across, populated by boulders and white water, led to a quiet, curving run where the gradient leveled off. The run is about one hundred feet long. A marsh bordered its right side. An island of gravel, sand, and tangled dead falls bordered its left. The run jogged in the middle, changing course from a northerly direction to an easterly direction. The water above the jog runs about two feet deep and the water below three to four feet. In the past, this run usually gave up, at most, several decent fish, usually rainbows.

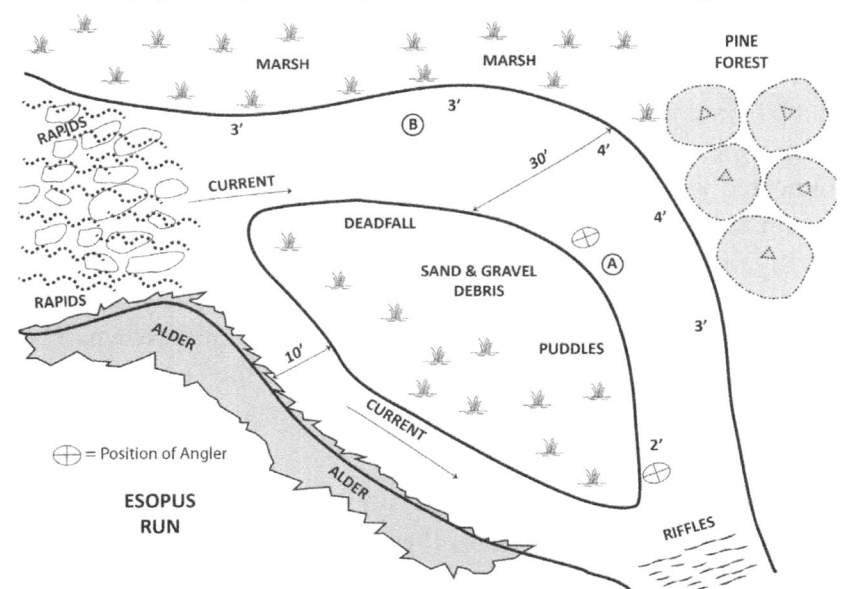

Wading upstream, fishing my Blue Winged Olive, I caught a few small trout. Approaching the run, I took up a casting position on its left side. Sticking with the Blue Winged Olive, I cast to Point A. Only a few curious looks and a tentative rise. Then came a size sixteen Quill, and after that, a size fourteen Gordon. Nothing. Then I changed to a size twelve high floating medium shade Dark Cahill. Cast after cast floated drag-free and took rainbow after rainbow. Even the first dozen I caught did not raise the suspicions of the dozen or so trout holding in the deeper water. More casts and a half-dozen more rainbows. Finally, when my casts brought no further rises, I moved to the bend of the jog still on the left side of the run. There, casting to Point B, another dozen trout fell to the medium shade high floating Dark Cahill. When the action trailed off, I wandered up to the foot of the rapids. It was there I saw the possible explanation for the frantic activity in the run. Slate Drake spinners hung above the rapid. Very likely, the medium Dark Cahill was close enough in color to be the effective fly that day.

# 9

## Ham Sandwiches with Neyle

Last night a late winter storm swept over the Catskills dropping a foot of snow along the course of the Neversink River. Sunrise, the storm clouds fled trailing a gilt-edged cold which brightened to a penetrating blue by noon. The cold arrested every creek cascading off Slide Mountain, fixing in place each plunge and cataract. Downstream at Claryville, Neversink Village, and Bradley, drifting snow buried trap lines and deer trails. Gasping misted vapors, the Neversink froze over. And so too froze the uneasy air eddying about the Knight house. Crystalled snowflakes pecked against my second-floor bedroom window warning me to stay inside. I needed no warning.

A single misjudgment, a twenty-year-old financial mistake, forced me to these cold mountains. It began in negligence. For that sin, Savannah banished Mother and me, a harsh sentence we are still serving. I alone was responsible for putting us in jeopardy. The history of the debacle still torments me, and I yearn for forgiveness. There will be none, for I do not know who could pronounce absolution.

Bright with mid-day sunlight, my tying table is littered with envelopes stuffed with feathers and hackles. Coughing, I lean over dripping more red splashes onto Jeanie's newspapers. The coughing escalates, the dry retching begins. My brows and palms grow clammy, and I slump forward, my whole frame trembling.

My breath returns. Time to start again. Sometimes I resent the perfection I demand of myself. It is more than my customers need. Fishing flies as with mayflies are things of the moment. Most gone before the end of summer. No matter, so much of my life, even the most fleeting, I task with perfection. I have no choice in the matter. It is who I am.

So many of the envelopes on my tying table came from Savannah. Milliners' return addresses. Mme. Louisa DesBoullion, Krouskopf, and others lining Broughton Street. Reading them, I hear Broughton Street's bustle, and feel its warmth. Our time in Savannah was a short lived idyll. In 1893, the national rail system collapsed bringing about the collapse of the Nation's financial markets. They called it a Panic. Overcapitalized and overbuilt with too many competing roads, railroad company after railroad company went into receivership, and the banks holding their debt failed with them. Capital scarce, efforts to consolidate and refinance the roads foundered and their worth plummeted. The Central of Georgia, where Mother and I invested most of our money, stayed solvent, and we felt secure in its regular dividends. It was false confidence. Lulled by its years of prudent management, I failed to perceive the Central's one great weakness. It was indispensable to forming a new, profitable southern railway system. The Central of Georgia alone served the port of Savannah and the port of Savannah exported most of Georgia's cotton. Cotton was selling well on foreign markets. So while railroads all over the south fell into insolvency, the Central of Georgia remained profitable.

When the railroad bubble burst, northeastern financiers hoarded their money. From afar they watched the bankrupt railroads of the South die off and waited until their value plummeted to scrap. Only New York money, J. P. Morgan and his allies, could afford the scrap, and when the value of the roads could sink no lower, they began to buy. The Central of Georgia held out. Before long, state and federal, judicial and political forces joined with Wall Street to put the Central into receivership. Later the court sold it out of receivership piece by piece wiping out most of its common stock holders. Mother and I among them. By the end of the decade, New Yorkers owned most of the South's railroads. Some of the New Yorkers who engineered our ruin now buy my flies.

Distressed with the prospect of living poor in Savannah, Mother left for South Orange, New Jersey. Our relatives, the Spencers, put her up in their coach house apartment. For a few years I hung on in Savannah hoping the Central would recover its independence, and we, our equity. Taking a less expensive apartment on Abercorn Street, I kept my Drayton Street office open. Solitary most days, I busied myself with a few short hours of paying business and many long hours of personal correspondence. Some mornings I visited the Central's offices for information. The clerks were tight lipped. Some days I wandered the Cotton Exchange fielding grim rumors. The growing number of well-dressed beggars on Broughton Street led me to believe my future held the worst. The only course open to me was working for an uncle on Wall Street, so I decided to follow Mother north. Nothing left to do but make my good-byes known to our Savannah relatives and friends.

The year of the Panic, Josephine Habersham died. She was buried in Laurel Grove Cemetery. Shuffling along in the line of mourners, I offered Neyle my condolences. The words were my own and after formally delivering them, Neyle, appreciative, said, "I hope to see you again at Avon."

"When you feel up to it," I said somberly.

Months passed with Neyle in seclusion. He was missing from Bay Street, the yacht club and Savannah's luncheon clubs. In spring a letter from him summoned me to Avon, "A few matters we should discuss." So the next Saturday, I again rode the White Bluff Road to Avon. No bass fishing, no dinner wit, just Neyle and me sitting closeted in his study. On the marquetry credenza were more dusty bottles of Madeira and a platter of ham sandwiches.

Shriveled and unkempt, in a wrinkled white shirt, sleeves rolled up, Neyle poured a glass, "This is a dry Madeira, one of my best blends." He sipped, "Yes." Then he poured a second glass and handed it to me. "Mostly a sercial grape but with a little bual for color."

"A beautiful amber." I sipped, "A crisp taste, like a sweet fall apple picked after the frost. Effervescent even."

"I have been following the Central of Georgia's problems. But there is so little solid information. You and your mother were heavy investors. What do you see coming?"

"I fear it will be gobbled up by northern interests." Swirling my glass, I watched the viscous liquid mount, drain and then settle, leaving a thin gold film high up the sides, "Mother and I will be gobbled up with it."

"I'm sorry."

"I appreciate your concern. So much of my life here is coming to an end. Mother's left for New Jersey." I hesitated and said in a lower register, "And Josephine is gone."

Neyle sat back and said wistfully, "We were a great duet." A light breeze carried the sweet scent of Josephine's carefully tended camellias, azaleas, and Japanese plums through the study windows. Neyle sniffed and was transported. "Her gardens remind me of her every hour of every day." Subdued, he whispered, "Last fall, one evening at the very end, she asked me to take her out one last time on the Vernon. The servants helped us into a small sail boat. Settling herself in the bow, Josephine handed me a piece of paper, 'I brought William's new poem. Would you read it to me?'"

'Putting my glasses on, I smoothed the paper on my knee and read it through aloud. I best remember Josephine's face, young once again, when I read,

*This beauteous inland stream*

*A thousand rills in soft harmonious flow*

*Run trickling through the main,*

*And join in voices sweet and low...*

"As I finished, Josephine looked about, listening to the last explosive clamor of evening bird call before twilight hushed all but the frogs and crickets. She stared long at the sluggish river and its border of green marsh grasses, banded tan and scarlet. And with a faint rise and fall of her breast, she savored the marsh air and smiled, "It is so complete out here. So perfect"'

Then fully self-possessed, she said, "'Thank you, Neyle. Time for me to go home."

Neyle stared into his glass. "The amber has a depth to it. Does it not?"

"Yes." As was Neyle's way, these words were but a rune stone planted in a vast, rich land of meaning he dared not explore for fear of losing his composure.

'That night sitting beside her I heard her hum, "Nearer my God to Thee." Not long after she died. In the quiet of her death, I read aloud her poem "The Star and the Flower" several times and lingered on the last lines "Let faith and hope the dew-drops be, That mirror heaven's light to thee."'

Neyle drew himself up and said firmly, "Every day I think on faith and hope and see her reflection on the veranda, doing lessons with our children and grandchildren, weeding and pruning in the garden perspiring in the mud and the heat. I see her....." Neyle drew himself up and said firmly, "I see her reflection testing the keys of her Rosewood piano before beginning a Beethoven piece. I hear her singing…'sweet and low'…singing…' He exhaled and slumped, his eyes dampening, "Singing…'sweet and low'…"

We sat silent together. Neyle's flute lay out on his desk. His fingers reached out but thinking better of it, drew back. "Sorry… What will you do if you're wiped out?"

"When it's clear we've lost everything, I'm going north, sir. An uncle, one of my father's relations, the Pecks, have offered me a place to stay and a job with his Wall Street firm. He has been very generous to us."

"In the end all you have is family. Could I offer a word of advice?"

"Please, sir. You've been like a father to me. I would be happy for it."

"At the end of the War, my finances were flat. Little cotton and less rice. My mills were in shambles. My two oldest sons died in the Battle for Atlanta. We were in mourning. A terrible time. What saved us were the Madeira pipes I hid from Sherman."

"I plan to work and save money for new investments. This time I'll put my money in bonds."

"Please understand me, Theodore. I prospered after the War because I put my trust in goods. Scarce commodities. Not pieces of paper. Fortunately I had the reputation for having the most precise palate in America, and I exploited that reputation. I developed new Madeira blends. Rainwater, Hurricane, Painted Pipes, All Saints and so on. Men with money, wealthy men, northerners and Europeans, paid my price for them. And this is the point, Theodore. My prosperity comes from owning goods that I produced according to my own secret formulas.

"I do not have your precise palate."

"You have a precise sense of color and line. I have seen it in the flies you tie. Think hard on this. I hold secret the ingredients of every one of my Madeira blends. The proportions of the grape varieties, the amount of brandy added, the temperatures at which the pipes are stored and the length of time they are stored, all different, all secret. Do you now understand? If you own scarce, desirable, secretly produced goods, it does not matter what the financial markets do. The wealthy always want something so rare only the very few can afford it." He chuckled, "Like the poor, the wealthy are always with us. They will pay you to keep your secrets. The greater the secret, the more they pay you."

"I'll think on it, sir."

"Please do, Theodore. I have grown fond of you and your

mother and worry about you both. If you ever need money, you can call on me."

Neyle's generosity touched me. "It is my problem, sir. For now I'm making my expenses."

"Theodore, after the War, so many of my friends, wealthy people with slaves and plantations lost everything but their lands. They launched new businesses but all their business schemes came to nothing, for they rested on cheap labor, a mindset they inherited from their parents. An archaic strategy." He took a sip of Madeira and held it up to the light. "Every one of their businesses failed, leaving them poorer than before."

Neyle's bluntness surprised me. He was rarely critical. "I've never depended on others, and I never intend to," I said.

Neyle leaned forward, his face flush with concern. "What I'm trying to impress on you Theodore, is that their mindset had no future. Failure was inevitable. It does not matter if you're independent. That is beside the point. Rethink your assumptions. You might be better off giving up some of your independence. I'm not saying you should. I'm just saying that you must challenge the mindset that brought you to this pass." He paused and ever so kindly said, "It's not working."

My reply did little more than fill the gap in our conversation. Another "Of course, sir" to tell Neyle I was listening and to admit our conversation had traveled beyond the limits of my own self-knowledge.

"What I worry most about, Theodore, is that your hopes, your vision of the future will become the playthings of survival. It is so hard to come back from that, to recover your dreams, to start afresh after you've jettisoned all just to survive."

Neyle did not expect a reply. I was alarmed and could do no more than whisper, "Thank you." With that Neyle picked up his flute and played a slow Vivaldi piece. The coda died in cold of Bradley. Captured by reverie, I tasted once again ham sandwiches washed down with Madeira. My fingers worked ahead on their own, tying familiar fly patterns by rote. Only the craving for a cigarette stilled them, dismissing both Avon and Neyle. Stiff, I sat back. I had been tying flies all day.

# 10

## My Uncle's Wall Street Office

My uncle's office radiated a staid reserve, a reflection of his calm determination. A relative from my father's side, William Peck was well off, a shrewd investor with liquid capital. After the Panic all manner of businessmen came to him for loans. They were in a rush. They wanted to get right down to business. Peck did not. His money was safe. His office vestibule became the anteroom to prudent discussion, the eye of the needle through which the financially needy must pass before their audience with him. During the wait, supplicants were expected to contemplate their great sin, indebtedness. After admitting the error of their ways, they were expected to marshal cold fact, to marry these facts to dignified language, and then to persuasively invent on Uncle Peck's capital a profitable future and an end to their indebtedness.

On Wall Street, I took on the role of an earnest clerk, serious, deferential, handling all with dispatch. Peck's mission was to make money, to build savings, to accumulate capital. He did not specialize. He bought and sold stocks, bonds and real estate, and for a fee he managed a few client accounts. Once discussing with me a client's woes, he fixed me and said, "By the time he came to me it was too late. He should have diversified. A rule you should have followed in Savannah." With the Panic, some of his tenants, especially his commercial tenants were slow to pay. They kept hoping the economy would turn up. I killed their hope communicating my uncle's *ultimata* in delicate prose.

And then I began to spit blood. My uncle worried, and the clerks complained that I spit blood on the floor of our common office. To stay in favor, I worked longer hours and ran more errands saving money by walking Lower Manhattan's fetid, crowded streets, streets where so many others also left their bloody sputum. Not long after I developed bronchitis and when the cough hung on, my mother intervened and insisted my uncle order me to a doctor. One morning he handed me a note with a doctor's name and address. "See to it." I looked up questioningly. "Now!" He ordered.

The cure was cold, pine scented mountain air. Peck's doctor followed the work of Drs. Trudeau and Loomis, two New York doctors, consumptives themselves, who extolled the benefits of living in the Adirondacks. Consumption arose from a bacillus which invaded the lungs. Healthy mountain air put the bacillus in remission and allowed the lungs to heal. Peck's doctor prescribed me ergot and instructed me to take a dose every few hours until my sputum no longer showed blood. For my night sweats, he prescribed quinine and elixir of vitriol.

"The drugs do some good but their effect is temporary. The only real cure is mountain air, a wholesome diet, and light exercise. At the Cottage Sanatorium on Saranac Lake, you'll get all three. Just a year should be enough to work the cure."

"I don't have the money to spend a year in the Adirondacks unemployed."

The doctor frowned, disappointed. "Then you might want to consider the Loomis Sanatorium for Consumptives. It's located in the Catskills, the town of Liberty to be exact, just a few hours from Manhattan by train. It's less expensive, and they have good people."

"Money is still an issue. My mother is an invalid, and I support her."

"You could try living in the Catskills summers and return to Manhattan for the winter. A half measure, but better than working year round in the city. You'll be dead in a few years if you keep going the way you're going. You'll be of no use to your mother then."

My uncle, an energetic man of florid complexion, took my report, impatiently, "Well what are you going to do?" He leaned forward resting his arms on his desk. His eyes softened. "I could give you time off during the summer. The worst part is you are your mother's favorite nurse. While you're absent, she'll be pestering us the whole time. She'll insist on joining you."

"I'll take a few days off to get my fever and coughing under control. Then I'll return here, put in full days again and start planning for summer." I bought a sputum cup and when the bloody cough returned a month later, I used it instead of spitting on the floor. The other clerks were grateful.

That spring, I rode the O&W north to Liberty. After investigating the sanatorium, I decided it was not for me because its regimen did not allow me the freedom to fish and tie flies. So I did what so many other consumptives did and took rooms at the Liberty House hotel, free to wander from river to river on my own schedule. I shall never forget the hotel's roast prime rib, creamed pearl onions and dilled cucumber slices in a vinaigrette dressing. At the end of the summer, the earnest clerk again, I returned tanned and healthy to Wall Street with a short term plan of spending winters in Manhattan and summers in the mountains. Uncle Peck approved of my plan and took over managing what was left of Mother's and my investments. The understanding was that any earnings would go first for Mother's care and the surplus, if any, to me. I started saving money and with it Uncle Peck made more investments for us.

Long term, my tuberculosis would force me to move to the Catskills permanently. I foresaw that and planned for it. One obstacle stood in the way, earning a regular income while living in the country. Never strong enough for physical work, I thought back to Habersham and tying flies. Since leaving Savannah I tied salmon flies for Neyle's friends. They paid well for standard English patterns. Once Neyle advised me to invent my own. This advice I ignored because my salmon fly patterns would have no pedigree. I had no experience salmon fishing. But his advice gave me an idea. Once established in the Catskills, I could build a pedigree for my own trout flies.

The summers in the Catskills demanded a new guise. No longer the diligent Wall Street clerk during summers, I sought a model from my bookshelf. Halford. His writings promoting scientific angling and dry fly fishing were just coming into favor with wealthy American trout fishers. So I went about the Catskills fashioning myself as the American Halford, courteous, remote, knowledgeable. In all ways superior.

At first my choice worked well. I knew Halford's mind. He was recruiting missionaries to spread the good news of dry fly fishing in America, and as a gift he sent me a full set of his own hand tied flies. Overwhelmed I signed up to preach the dry fly gospel repeating to all who would listen Halford's divine *dicta*. What I had not counted on was that Halford's dry flies did not catch our American trout. And so my loyalty to Halford and scientific angling secretly withered. I became an apostate without mentioning my change of heart to Halford's American disciples, my best customers.

My guise as the American Halford was never a perfect fit. There were unbridgeable differences between us. Money was of little concern to Halford, a successful industrialist, early retired. One of a few dozen members of England's exclusive Houghton Fly Fishers club, Halford fished private waters on the Test, the Itchen and the Berkshire Kennet, three of England's most exclusive chalk streams. In character the three rivers were the same, all brown trout and grayling, all prolific, clear, slow moving, regular in every way, from the pace of the currents to the emergence dates of its mayflies, caddis, and stoneflies.

I was a pretender to wealth. By slights of hand in the Catskills, I took on the character of a successful semi-retired Wall Street stock broker caught up in the dry fly craze. The fraud masked the harsh truths of my thin wallet. I could hardly afford the few fly rods I owned and had no money to join a private fishing club. Instead I fished the public waters of the Catskill, fast moving rivers. Brown trout, some of good size, did thrive in the Catskills, but unlike the British chalk streams, conditions in the mountains changed markedly from day to day and year to year.

Halford's greatest attribute, his generosity of mind, was beyond me. My purpose from the start was to establish my reputation as the Catskills' premier fly fisher. Building a reputation takes time. Years of fishing. Years of keeping up with fishing literature. Years of catching the biggest trout and letting others know about it. And most importantly, years of never letting on to others the secrets of my success. My customers and I fished the same rivers. I could only become a celebrity if I succeeded where others failed. They did fail. And my heart hardened watching them fail.

To advertise my reputation beyond New York, I wrote. Not books like Halford but short articles. The wealthiest American fly fishers subscribed to *The Field* and *The Fishing Gazette,* both British sports magazines. Upon Halford's recommendation, the *Gazette's* editor, Robert Marston, named me the *Gazette's* American correspondent.

Enough of my consumption.

Enough of Halford.

In the dark before falling asleep, the day passes before me. It was a good day. The highlight, two visitors, Bruce LeRoy in the morning and Roy Steenrod, in the afternoon.

Bruce brought me a glossy red rooster. Bruce and I are partners in a hackle business. I purchase the chickens, and Bruce breeds them. We hope to develop chickens with perfect hackle colors, especially dun and sandy dun hackles. For the duns, we cross Andalusian Blues with lighter grays, gingers and Plymouth Rocks. As I remind Bruce, the goal is hackle "the color of water." If we are successful, the business could become global. The prospect excites Bruce, and he named one of his sons after me.

Immediately the red headed rooster made problems for Jeanie. It tore up the newspapers she had scattered under my tying table.

At my urging she fetched more newspapers and covered the whole floor. I murmured something about changing the newspapers every day as well as providing a pouch of cracked corn and a bowl of water for my noble friend.

Jeanie replied under her breath, "Chickens belong in coops." But shortly she brought water and a pouch of corn.

Bruce shook out a few kernels. Dropping them in my palm, he said, "Pat your leg, Mr. Gordon." I did, and the rooster flew up and stood on my knee cocking its head this way and that scrutinizing me. We all laughed, even Jeanie.

"Now feed it the corn and stroke its head as if you were looking for a hackle," Bruce said.

The rooster stood still for my examination, and for a test I pulled a hackle out. My noble friend did not flinch. More kernels and I set it back down where it strutted about ruffling its wings and muttering.

In the afternoon Roy Steenrod, Liberty's postal clerk, brought my mail, a dozen letters. On top one from Dr. Griffin. An easy order very likely. I expected news of a visit from my mother, but no letter from South Orange. Since 1906 it was Mother's and my routine to take rooms at the Liberty House during the winter where it fell to me to nurse, bathe, and dress her. Come spring, she would leave for South Orange, while I convalesced to regain my strength. No letter meant she was not strong enough for the short trip to Liberty. It worried me.

The rooster clucked when Roy entered. "You have a new roommate I see." I patted my leg and my noble friend jumped up again on my knee. Roy smiled. Slipping out a hackle, I gave it to him, "For your next fly."

"Thank you. Time to start tying for Opening Day," Roy said saluting me with the small brandy I set out for him. During winter I served brandy to my visitors, "to take the chill off." A ritual, my local friends came to expect. I joined Roy with a small glass of my own.

"My customers come first, Mr. Steenrod." I did not let on that this winter just tying for my customers sapped all my strength.

"Mother has a taste for speckled trout. I'm thinking of tying a few gaudy, sunk flies for Opening Day. Fancy flies to flash in the dark, roiled water."

"Fancy flies worked for me before the brown trout and the dry fly bacillus."

"I'm thinking of going dry fly once the run offs over," Roy said. "But for now I want a big bright fly. Any favorite pattern, Mr. Gordon?"

"The fancy flies I fished, you'll find in Mary Orvis' book. Get my copy from the book shelf by the window."

"Just one or two bright ones. My time is short after I get off work. I want to knot on one fly and leave it on all evening."

True to my bent, I did not discourage him. Often enough I told Roy to fish the fly that fits the needs of the moment. The custom work big fish demand. Free advice never makes much of an impression. No need to repeat myself. Only more fishing will put him right. Instead I tell him what he wants to hear, "Worth a try." Trial and error taught me everything I know about fly fishing because it taught me the how of coming to a successful solution. Trial and error, new trials and more errors, and finally a trial producing a small truth. Fishing a bright fly to brown trout is an oft duplicated trial which ends mostly in failure.

Roy pulled Mary Orvis' book off the shelf. "If you don't mind, I'll borrow it for a few weeks. I'm thinking of a Parmachene Belle. One of the city people raved about it last summer."

"Take it." Orvis' book did illustrate the Parmachene Belle pattern. "Nothing like seeing a speckled trout break the surface with a Belle in its jaw," I said between sips. In truth the Belle was a North Woods fly which brought me little luck even on the teeming brook trout creeks plunging down Slide Mountain. I needed Roy's companionship more than I needed a grateful protégée.

Roy nodded, "Well, I won't take up any more of your time, Mr. Gordon. I'm expected at home."

"Roy, if you see Christian, tell him I forgot to give him the Marble gaff and steel stringer I promised him. They're hanging there," I said pointing to the back of the door to my room. "He catches the biggest fish so he needs them."

Roy hesitated, then looked down, his soulful eyes following the strutting rooster. When they lighted on the red splotches staining the newspapers beneath my tying table, he said, "Of course, Mr. Gordon."

"And don't mind the fawning fat lady, Mr. Steenrod when you leave. She's been tippling my bourbon again and gushes over visitors."

Roy brightened, "Of course not, Mr. Gordon."

The murmur of "good byes" between Roy and Jeanie reached me through the grate of the register my room shares with the kitchen. Roy is one of Jeanie's favorites.

After Roy left, I read Dr. Griffin's letter. An old customer, he fishes Michigan's Au Sable River. In the early days the Au Sable was a grayling river. Any fancy fly worked. In those days the doctor's favorite patterns were the Professor, the Montreal, and any other wet fly concoction splashing yellows and reds, silvers and golds. The Michigan grayling was a trusting fish. Too trusting. I say "was." In a generation they disappeared, and the Au Sable became a brook and brown trout river and now by law can only be fished with artificial flies. My dull creations bring brook and brown trout to Dr. Griffin's net. A fan of Halford and scientific angling, he ordered dry flies, one dozen each of the Dark Cahill, the Quill Gordon and the Gordon.

With Dr. Griffin's letter came a money order, enough to cover Anson's board and room for two weeks. The Dark Cahills I will tie at my table using a vice and hackle from my noble rooster's top knot. Afterwards, I will recline on my bed, elevate my legs, and tie the Gordons and Quill Gordons by hand. These days my ankles swell when I stand or sit up too long. At the speed with which I have been tying lately, it will be dark before I finish.

Dr. Griffin's note inquired of my health, a subject I refuse to discuss with anyone but my doctors at Loomis. Insistent coughing and bloody sputum tell the story. I will fill Dr. Griffin's order and mail it off tomorrow with a note recommending a dozen Whirling Duns for the Au Sable's brown trout. He will order them, and I will earn more money.

On Opening Day, Dr. Griffin stays at the Douglas House on the North Branch of the Au Sable, "an old man's river" as he describes it in his letters. Mostly thigh high, mostly packed gravel, level walking, submerged weed clumps and cedar sweepers shunt the broad river into separate channels, each an intimate stream flowing at a moderate pace within the broad river. A much different river from my Neversink. Above Bradley, the Neversink is a young man's river bounding from boulder to boulder, catapulting over stone ledges. Nearing Bradley it broadens, running through riffles, quick rapids and slow deep pools, some very deep. In the rapids, every year, powerful currents sweep away tottering anglers, drowning some. When the Neversink runs high and dark with snow melt, I take Herman Christian, along as my wading staff. With all the snow on the mountains this year, I will need him this Opening Day.

Among the locals Christian, as I call him, is my favorite. He tolerates me best. He sees people as from a great height. With bemused indifference, he looks past my stiff formalities, my irritability, and my sarcasm toward all things rural and northern. Unlike Roy, my on again, off again days do not bother him. And they should not. I am moody, that is all, just moody. Christian accepts my moods, humoring me, wryly smiling when I rant, blithely ignoring any pointed criticisms when I lose patience with him. In the Philippines, he earned the calm only battle tested soldiers display. While living in the South, I encountered the same unshakable equanimity in aged Confederate soldiers, for the most part front line infantry and officers.

Returning home from a frustrating day on the Neversink, silently wrapped in thought, I would run down my checklist wondering where I went wrong. Hardly aware of the path, stumbling now and again, the sound of Christian's regular tramp and occasional helping hand guided me home. Before turning off, he would say by way of goodbye, "Tomorrow will be different."

Never moved by his optimism, I scolded him, "But why?"

"You'll figure it out," he would say grinning at me sideways.

Occasionally my suspicions pressed me to wonder what Christian saw in me. I did not know, and never asked doubting he could have told me. What I did sense was his firm confidence in me as an angler, and that was enough.

As expected of fly fishers these days, our trips together are mounted as scientific expeditions. Halford started the fad. In that spirit, Christian hired on as my laboratory assistant. By the time the Knights put me up in their second floor room, Christian and I were a seasoned research team. On one matter I depart from Halford. As you might expect, I never keep laboratory notes. Better left to memory, safe from prying eyes.

Of late Christian does my fishing. I string my rod, affix a fly, usually an experimental tie, and hand it to him. He casts better than I; he is more patient than I; and most importantly he has the breath to support my stubbornness. It is a joy watching him. My flies are lucky to have him, for he gives them a better showing than I can these days.

For years I played the two faced game with Roy and Christian. They wanted my flies but had no money to pay for them. I wanted feathers and someone to deliver my mail. It was a good trade. After Roy and Christian dissected my flies, they tied their own bringing them to me for appraisal. Usually I gave them a cursory glance, made a suggestion, and then handed them back saying, "It should catch fish." At some time or other every fly will catch a fish. They tarried to talk, and in time they believed me their friend.

That was all to the good. Yet I could not let it be. As is the way of country youth, Roy and Christian are rivals. They boast to each other about the points of their bucks, about the number of wood cords they cut, about the grouse and woodcock shot on the wing, and about the size and number of their fish. Shameful to say I fostered this rivalry. Out of fear. I feared they would grow tired of me after learning all that I knew about fly tying and fly fishing. At first I never fathomed how much they enjoyed talking to me about my life, about the great world beyond Liberty, about my thoughts on the war in Europe, about Savannah and the South, the man Halford, the man Skues, the weather, and Jeanie Knight. That my companionship seemed enough for them made me suspicious.

Staring up at the ceiling, I say to no one, "I'm sorry." No doubt I goaded their rivalry. Praising Roy to Christian on his fly tying and never complimenting Christian on his. Praising Christian's angling skills to Roy and never complimenting Roy on his. I revealed just so much to them and no more, two straight forward young men.

The silence lengthens out. It chastens me. "They do not deserve my treatment of them," I murmur into the dark. Unwelcome, Habersham's advice comes back, "Your value lies in the value of the secrets you hold." But Habersham never warned me that my secrets would feed my loneliness. Holding onto secrets drives me apart from others. The deeper the secrets, the more bitter the loneliness. So I relent. Tomorrow I will suggest Roy and Christian tie both Cahills and my Quill sparse and fish them in the film. Jettisoning that secret should relieve my loneliness somewhat.

At night drifting off to sleep, I am on the Neversink watching myself as I cast a single wing sparse version of my Quill up and across. I watch it float down in the surface film and at the moment it begins to swing I pull it under releasing a handful of line to allow it to carry on down farther dead drift. And then when it begins to swing again, I tease it to the surface, let it sink back, and then work it back deliberately as a living insect. And with that vision I fall asleep.

## 11

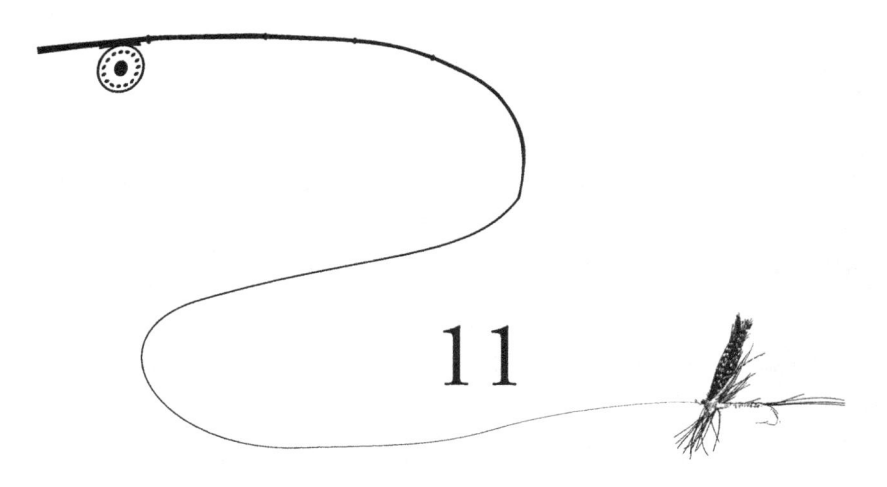

## Favorite Flies

    Prying anglers annoy me. They want to know where I fish, when I fish, the names of my favorite flies, and, worse, they want all this information for free. Prying anglers do not expect to consult lawyers or doctors for free, but because fishing is, they believe, a frivolous pursuit and unworthy of their full attention, they pester successful anglers like myself instead of reading and experimenting for themselves. Their questions anger me because they show a lack of respect, an utter disregard for the work it takes to become a competent fly fisher. I have put in that work and so earned all I know of fly fishing for trout. They have not. They want something for nothing, and they think me such a fool that I will hand it over without hesitation. So I resent them. Meeting such anglers on the river, I become disagreeable, evading their questions and making up excuses for immediately ending further conversation. It is all the civility I can muster.

    One August day last summer, Anson and I went upriver to fish the pool below York's Ford. As usual, Anson brought worms, and as usual, I caught more and bigger fish on flies. After a few hours, we had the night's supper and the morrow's breakfast.

    On the way back to Bradley, Anson chuckled, "Most of the neighbors here about complain that you're the rudest man for miles."

"I'll not deny it."

Anson shot me a glance. "In your defense, I tell them you're cantankerous."

"I'm that too."

"Most of them irritate me," Anson said. "Lyin' about what they shoot, catch, trap, and grow." He slapped the reins. "It's hard to say a kind word to a braggart."

"For me, it's worse. It's condoning a crime. They're attempting to steal from me, and I'll not become an accessory to my own impoverishment."

Breezily, Anson replied, "I'll never pester you about what flies to use. My choice is always garden hackle."

"Truth be told, I do not have a set list of favorite flies, Anson." Tapping a finger to my head, I said, "I keep a list of my most frequently carried flies up here. For now, that list is short on names and long on shades."

Nature shows all colors and all shades of color. I am biased on this point. The rationale supporting my bias is found in the theory of mimicry which holds that colors are borrowed between natural species and kingdoms for defense and procreation purposes. As I interpret this theory, the fly tier is assured he will find the perfect shades for imitating insects in the plumage of birds and the fur of mammals. If fly tiers are missing the right color, they need only inspect bird skins and animal pelts until the perfect color comes to hand. And it has been my experience that it always come to hand. Halford and his scientific anglers find their colors and shades in dye pots. Doing so is expensive and misses the subtleties of nature's colors.

I have collected dozens upon dozens of bird skins to imitate insect legs, wings, and body colors. The list includes: Adjutant, American Bittern, Blackbird, Bluebird, Blue Grouse, Blue Jay, Bustard, Canvasback Duck, Capercaillie, California Condor, Coot, Curlew, Egyptian Goose, Flicker, Fieldfare, Golden Pheasant,

Green Parrot, Guinea Fowl, Gull, Heron, Kingfisher, King Rail, Mallard Duck, Marsh Hen, Partridge, Peacock and Pea Hen, Plover, Red Headed Duck, Ring Neck Pheasant, Robin, Ruffed Grouse, Scarlet Ibis, Snipe, Starling, Teal, Turkey, Widgeon, Wood Duck, and Woodcock. Peacock eyes, the green and the blue, are especially important, for they lend lighter and darker banding for my Quill.

Where possible, I substitute dubbed fur for a fly's body. To achieve the right color, I collected boxes of pelts: Ermine, Fox, Hare skins with masks, Mink (summer and winter), Mole (American and Irish), Muskrat, Polar Bear, Raccoon, Rabbit, Rat, Squirrel skins and tails (Fox, Gray and Red), Seal, and Weasel. Very early, I left off using horse hair, Halford's favorite material for fly bodies. It lends itself to dying. Instead, I substitute dubbed fur. It catches more fish.

Most of the fly tying materials I use are generally available. When tying my own flies, I rarely travel beyond local farmyards and marshes. Chickens, grouse, muskrat, fox, hare, sheep, wood duck, and mallard duck answer most of my needs. The only exotic material, peacock eyes, are sold locally by milliners and dry good shops. Through Bruce LeRoy's breeding program, I am never short hackle in black, red/brown, grizzly, ginger, and white colors. It is another story for dun hackle, my favorite color, especially sandy dun hackle in small sizes. Useful dun hackle is always in short supply.

Anglers who spend time with me could make up a list of my most used flies. Certainly Christian, Bruce, and Roy could and no doubt so could Skues, for my letters to him discuss them and their dressings. Now to the list of flies I carry at the present:

## Dark Cahill

The Dark Cahill, or Cahill as it was first known, enjoys a following in the Catskills. Benjamin Kent's essay "An Angler's Notes on the Beaverkill" included in Rhead's *The Speckled Brook Trout* (R. H. Russell 1902) listed the Cahill first of all the flies he recommended. "In my opinion the Cahill is the best fly on the Beaverkill; it was the best when I first fished the stream and it is the best today." He preferred a light shaded tie. I agree with him and carry it in light as well as medium and dark shades. Sizes #10 through #16, sparse and full hackle.

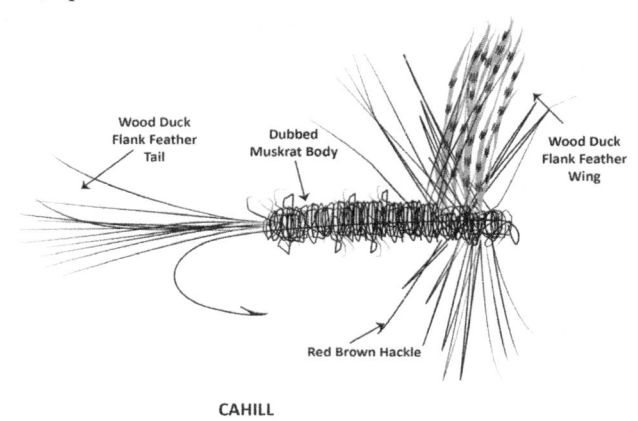

CAHILL

**Wing:** slips of dark wood duck flank feather, lighter wood duck flank feather, and very light well marked mallard flank feather to achieve the dark, medium, and light shades.

**Tail:** a very narrow slip of wood duck or mallard flank feather depending on shade seeking to achieve.

**Body:** dubbing from back of mature muskrat for dark, belly fur from very young muskrat or fox for medium, natural colored Icelandic sheep's wool for light.

**Hackle:** red/brown hackle in dark, medium, and light. Light Ginger and medium Red/brown mixed will substitute for light.

*Author's Note: For sparse ties, Chinese, Indian, or similar quality necks can be used if color is right and the hackle is stiff and glossy. They best simulate the hackle available to Gordon in his day.*

*Note 1: For winged sparse ties add no more than a single, narrow wing slanted backward.*

*Note 2: Darker wood duck flank feathers can be found on older birds; the medium on younger birds.*

## Light Cahill

The color progression of Light Cahill mayflies emerging over the summer starts in a light tan color in June, and as the summer progresses, the color tends to lighter and lighter shades of cream. Sizes #10 through #16, sparse and full hackle.

**Wing:** very light wood duck or mallard flank feather for darker shades in early summer and then to lighter yet for the appropriate later summer shades. Sometimes a very light young starling wing of a bright bluish color is effective.

**Tail:** narrow slip of wood duck or mallard flank feather depending on summer phase.

**Body:** light tan dubbing for dark, dark cream for medium, and fitch or fox belly for light.

**Hackle:** dark, medium, and light ginger.

*Note: Variously bleached muskrat is a good substitute for dark and medium Light Cahill dubbing.*

## Quill Gordon

Over several trout seasons, I tinkered with this pattern. By the spring of 1906, I was satisfied enough to mail off two specimens, one to Marston at the *Gazette* in April and the other to my then new correspondent, G. E. M. Skues, in May. Both specimens had similar stripped quill bodies. The one sent to Marston was tied with light dun hackles, a few sprigs of wood duck for the tail, and wood duck slips for the wings. The specimen sent to Skues was tied with light dun hackle, a few barbs of light dun hackle for the tail, and wood duck slips for the wings.

Dun is my keystone color. Of the dun colors, the sandy dun—a dun with hints of buff or pale yellow, two colors frequently found in nature—is the most useful. Over the years, I tied my Quill as well as my Gordon in honey dun, mottled dun, dark dun, pale dun, silver dun, pale blue dun, and steel blue dun. None work day in and day out as well as the sandy dun color in light, medium, and dark versions.

For myself, I tie the sparse and full versions of my Quill with no wings, a single wing, or a double wing, depending on conditions. Sometimes, I splay two slips of wood duck to suggest a spinner. The splayed version has been very effective on the Beaverkill, and its influence shows up in the Quills sold by Mills, the tackle manufacturer. The sparse tie with a single upright wing is my workhorse. I tie it only for my own use. Sizes #10 through #17, sparse and full.

**Wing:** wood duck flank feathers in shades of light, medium and dark depending on shade trying to achieve. For light version a well-marked mallard flank feather will do nicely.

**Tail:** wood duck flank feather slips or dun hackle barbs in needed shades.

**Body:** stripped peacock quill.

**Hackle:** sandy dun hackle in appropriate shades.

*Note 1: Varnish the hook shank before winding on the quill.*

*Note 2: Use stripped quill with strongly contrasting banding.*

*Note 3: Gold wire ribbing is optional.*

## Gordon

I first named this fly the Golden Brown Spinner (GBS). My customers refer to it as the Gordon, and that is the name that has stuck. It is a spinner that is at home above, in, or under the surface. I believe it is especially effective fished below the surface in smaller hook sizes, #14 through #16.

Initially, I tied it with a brown body and spoonbill wings. After experimentation, I settled on bodies of dark golden Flicker quills for the dark version and pale golden mohair dubbing for the lighter. Sizes #10 through #16, sparse and full.

**Tail:** a narrow slip of either dark or light wood duck flank feather depending on the shade.

**Wing:** dark or light wood duck flank feather depending on shade duplicating.

**Body:** flicker quills or gold colored mohair in shades. Dubbed ties are segmented using fine gold braid for both the dark and light gold dubbed mohair versions.

**Hackle:** badger hackle or sandy dun in dark and lighter shades.

## Beaverkill

I appropriated the British Silver Sedge from Halford and Francis Francis, merely changing its name to Americanize it. I did experiment with other ties and shades, coming up with a variation substituting stripped peacock quill for the white floss body. This version was surprisingly effective, so I give both dressings here. Another British pattern similar to the Beaverkill is the Wickham's Fancy, which I carry sometimes. I do not list it separately due to its limited use. Sizes #12 through #16, sparse and full.

**First Version**

**Wing:** dark dun hackle tips or landrail slips

**Tail:** brown hackle barbs

**Body:** white floss with silver wire ribbing

**Hackle:** brown hackle palmered

**Second Version**

**Wing:** wood duck flank feathers

**Tail:** honey dun hackle barbs

**Body:** stripped peacock quill

**Hackle:** honey dun palmered

*Note: At times, I tie this fly in both versions with a ginger hackle palmered.*

## Mink Fly

My brown caddis pattern I call the "mink fly." It apes the traditional English Brown Sedge. For the Catskills, it is most effective when tied with light summer mink dubbing. The lighter summer mink dubbing comes from the mink's flank and belly, a medium brown, almost a dark tan color. Sizes #12 through #17 in sparse and full.

**Wing:** brown hackle tips

**Tail:** brown hackle barbs

**Body:** summer mink fur dubbing

**Hackle:** medium brown hackle

*Note 1: Wings can be tied flat or upright. Caddis wings flap upright when they are lifting off or descending to the surface of the river as in ovipositing.*

*Note 2: I have experimented with different shades, yet now advocate light summer mink.*

## Grannom

The word grannom refers to more than one species of caddis. For me, it refers to two different caddis flies. The first is a small black caddis that appears in the spring. It is a very dark blue/black color. Its female carries an orange egg sac. A dark bluish dun-colored hackle from a Kingfisher is best. #17 sparse and full.

My other grannom is what I call the "good dun." It is a larger fly incorporating some green in the body. The basic dubbing is lighter hare's ear, to which snippets of green floss are added. Depending on how deep the green of the natural is, I will add more or less of the green floss snippets. The final effect is a dirty green. Most caddis hatching in May show green, some more than others. By varying the dubbing mix, these caddis can be closely imitated. Sizes # 12 through size #17, sparse and full.

## Grannom One

**Wing:** very dark dun almost a blue/black

**Tail:** very dark blue dun hackle barbs

**Body:** dark black dubbing with orange egg sac for female

**Hackle:** dark, dark dun, almost black (best from a Kingfisher)

## Grannom Two – The Good Dun

**Wing:** medium dun hackle tips or mallard flight feather slips

**Tail:** dark and light ginger hackle barbs

**Body:** a mix of very light hare's ear and snippets of green floss for a more or less dirty green.

**Hackle:** dark or light ginger

*Note 1: Hackle for both versions can be either palmered or wound on as a collar.*

*Note 2: It is best to use a standard medium green floss for the Good Dun.*

## Pale Evening Dun

I struggle with this fly dressing. Over the last ten years, I have fiddled with many different versions. For the time being, I do not see the point in nailing down the recipe. Ambiguity and imprecision are the fly fisher's constant challenge. I never settle on a fly dressing until I am absolutely certain. For the present, I carry four versions. To human perception, the natural is a vaguely pale yellow and light dun fly. The first three of my dressings show a cream slightly dun colored body with a hackle of either cream, sandy dun, or pale yellow. My fourth dressing calls for a decidedly pale yellow fly. It has a quill showing yellow from an onion skin bath or dubbed very light yellow mohair body with pale dun hackle and wings. The first three versions do not match the color of the natural in hand. The fourth does. On occasion, any of the four may be the effective fly. Sizes #12 through #17 in sparse and full.

**First Version**

**Wing:** pale dun hackle tips

**Tail:** either pale dun or light sandy dun hackle barbs

**Body:** very pale dun from fox belly fur

**Hackle:** sandy dun or pale dun with a yellowish cast, never olive.

**Second Version**

**Wing:** pale dun hackle tips

**Tail:** pale dun hackle barbs

**Body:** very pale dun fox or coyote belly fur

**Hackle:** cream

**Third Version**

**Wing:** bluish young starling slips or light dun hen hackle tips

**Tail:** pale dun barbs of a yellow cast

**Body:** the very lightest dun from cream fox

**Hackle:** pale sandy dun

**Fourth Version**

**Wings:** light dun hackle tips

**Tail:** light dun hackle barbs

**Body:** peacock quill dyed yellow in an onion skin bath or very pale yellow mohair dubbing

**Hackle:** very light sandy dun or light dun with a yellow cast

## Fan Wing Royal Coachman

I was the first to tie the Royal Coachman with white wood duck breast feathers for wings. I have recommended this dressing to Skues. Other species of duck breast feathers have been tried by others, many illustrated in Mary Orvis Marbury's book.

It is true I have disparaged fishing the Royal Coachman except for times when rivers run dark. The Fan Wing Royal is a different matter. It does catch large brown trout, and that alone is a good enough reason to carry it. Sizes #10 and #12. Full tie only.

**Wing:** identically matched white wood duck breast feathers

**Tail:** Golden Pheasant tippet

**Hackle:** red brown

**Body:** peacock herl with waist of red floss

*Note 1: Tying this fly on heavier hooks aids it to cock upright.*

*Note 2: If the wings are out of balance, this fly will spin in flight. Balance is achieved by using identical breast feathers. These are located near each other on the breast of the wood duck.*

## Black Gnat

I have modified the standard patterns for my own use. For the small ties, I generally follow Halford's dressing with some minor modifications. For the larger sizes, I recommend the standard tie found in Mary Orvis Marbury's book. As obvious from the dressing below, my changes are cosmetic. For the small sizes, I tie it full with the smallest hooks available. For the larger sizes, I recommend tied sparse with a single wing. Sizes #6 through #10 for large and Sizes #14 through #17 for small (sparse and full).

### Small Version

**Wing:** pale blue young starling, or pale dun hackle tips

**Tail:** black hackle barbs

**Body:** jet black ostrich quill with a silver tag

**Hackle:** dark starling

### Large Version

**Wing:** black duck, crow, or raven flight feather slip

**Tail:** a few black hackle barbs, short

**Body:** black chenille

**Hackle:** black

## Red and Ginger Quill

These can be fished as dark and light spinner patterns. Halford called the Red Quill "one of the sheet anchors of a dry fly fisherman on a strange river, when in doubt." Although I criticize Halford's dry fly orthodoxy, I take his fly recommendations seriously. This pattern has worked for me. Sizes #10 through #16, sparse and full.

## Red Quill

**Tail:** red brown hackle barbs

**Body:** Peacock quill in darker shade

**Hackle:** red brown hackle with a black center

## Ginger Quill

**Tail:** pale brownish ginger

**Body:** Peacock quill in lighter shade

**Hackle:** pale brownish ginger

## Beetles

I carry few terrestrials. For flying ants. my recipe goes as follows: lightest dun or red/brown hackles, starling wing, peacock herl body. Sometimes, I use this pattern as a searching fly in summer when rivers seem empty of fish.

Two beetle patterns I carry regularly. The first is a fairly typical black beetle pattern with its shell a black feather slip tied over its back. The other pattern is similar to the black version, but with a white feather slip, instead of a black, tied over the back. Sizes #14 and #16 sparse tie.

## Black Beetle

**Black Shell:** black feather folded from front to back and tied down at hook bend

**Body:** black Ostrich herl formed into a perfect circle

**Hackle:** black

## White beetle

**White Shell:** white feather folded over back and tied down at bend of the hook

**Body:** Peacock herl shaped into perfect circle

**Hackle:** dark red

## Crane Fly

When crane flies are active, I fish my own imitation. It will be difficult to cast in high winds, but is often worth the effort. Sizes #12 through #16 full tie.

**Wing:** grizzly hackle tips with clear bar markings

**Tail:** pale brown hackle barbs, over-sized

**Body:** brown raffia

**Hackle:** pale brown over-sized by two hook sizes more or less

## Gold Ribbed Hare's Ear

This fly troubles me. Halford called the Gold Ribbed Hare's Ear fly "the most successful of modern times." The fur hackled version was included with the four dozen flies he shipped me. I lost it before it proved useful. Years later, Skues sent me another specimen. Because of its notoriety, I tinkered with different ties for it throughout my life. It looks very similar on the water to the Wickham's Fancy, a fly I have used with success during caddis emergences. The dressings below have proved their worth often enough. Sizes #10 through #16, sparse and full.

### Version One

**Wing:** can add usually none but darker mallard dun slips or medium dun hackle tips

**Tail:** barbs from either a medium dun or grizzly hackle

**Body:** rough Hare's Ear fur with poll favoring brown, black, and gray colors, then ribbed with narrow flat gold tinsel

**Hackle:** slightly barred dark grizzly hackle

### Version Two

**Wing:** usually none but can add very light mallard or light dun hackle tips

**Tail:** light grizzly hackle barbs

**Body:** polls from Hare's Ears favoring tans, oranges, and white with narrow gold tinsel ribbing

**Hackle:** slightly barred light grizzly hackle or very light blue dun hackle

## Larva

The Larva is an early season fly I tie for Opening Day stream conditions. I have found its use is limited to fishing spring's high, dark, cold water when all else fails and the angler is tempted to worms. For a while, Christian and Roy called it the "pig fly" because I blended pig fur with red seal fur dubbing, simulating the pinkish color of the Tup's Indispensable. This a deeply sunk wet fly I tie in three shades. Sizes #6 through #12.

### Dressing

**Hackle:** dark dun hackle, steel blue hackle, light sandy dun hackle, all palmered

**Tail:** Ibis slip

**Body:** shades of body color running from light to dark from either muskrat, or hare's ear, and the Tup's Indispensable mix –

pig wool and red or claret seal fur dubbing blended to a bright pink

**Ribbing:** gold or silver tinsel

## Blue Winged Olive

The mayflies falling under this rubric are numerous and varied. I will never be dogmatic about the dressings for this pattern. It is best to experiment with various colors to match the species found on your home rivers. Of all the flies listed in this collection, this one involves the greatest guesswork. The dressing incorporates many of the values I look for in a killing fly—a dun colored hackle wing, segmentation, and a color matching the natural. This is one fly where comparisons in hand versus comparisons on the river make the difference between an effective fly and a dud. Sizes #14 through #17 sparse.

**Body:** dubbing to match the color of natural with the lower portion of body thinner than the thorax

**Ribbing:** very thin gold wire wound over the bottom half of fly

**Hackle:** light, dark, or sandy dun, depending on color of the natural

**Wing:** hackle wound over dubbed thorax three turns

**Tail:** dun hackle barbs, depending on the shade of the natural fly

## Bumblepuppy

The Bumblepuppy is one of three flies most closely associated with my name. The other two are, of course, the Gordon and the Quill Gordon. Of the three, the Bumblepuppy came first in 1903, the Gordon shortly afterwards, and the Quill in 1906. I sent a version of the Bumblepuppy to Marston. Christian has simplified the tie since and fishes it as a bucktail. He ties it with a white bucktail wing and a full yellow chenille body. My pattern is tied in three colors, black and white, yellow and white, and red and white. The red version is killing on Delaware River smallmouths. One day, I caught one hundred on it. The Bumblepuppy is both a dry and a wet fly. Sizes long shank #6 through #10.

**Tag:** silver tinsel and red silk

**Tail:** two mated Ibis slips back to back straight out behind the hook

**Butt:** red, yellow, or black narrow silk chenille

**Body:** white narrow silk chenille ribbed with narrow flat silver tinsel

**Hackle:** badger very full and long

**Wing:** white swan or goose over white bucktail, bear, or goat

**Sides:** jungle cock nails

**Shoulder Hackle:** overwing with Widgeon as long or longer than Badger hackle

**Head:** red, yellow, or black narrow silk chenille

*Note: The most attractive feature of this fly is its hackle, which expands at rest and contracts when pulled forward to imitate a darting minnow.*

The list of flies I carry ends here. Two other popular flies I originated and once carried are the Catskill and the La Branche. The dressing for the Catskill is very similar to the dressing for the Queen of the Waters, which uses teal for its wing. I substituted wood duck for the wing and a slip of wood duck for a tail. It imitates a large orange caddis. The La Branche is a fly I concocted and sent to La Branche to test. It is simply a gray fly in all its parts, very close to the Whirling Blue Dun. The name was affixed later by La Branche and his friends. My Quill tied in three shades will answer any angler's need for a dun-colored fly. I never sent La Branche a specimen of my Quill. Who knows what name he would have given it? He buys them at Mills where it is labeled the Quill Gordon. Once he did order them from me, and I charged him double Mills' price. He went back to Mills.

## 12

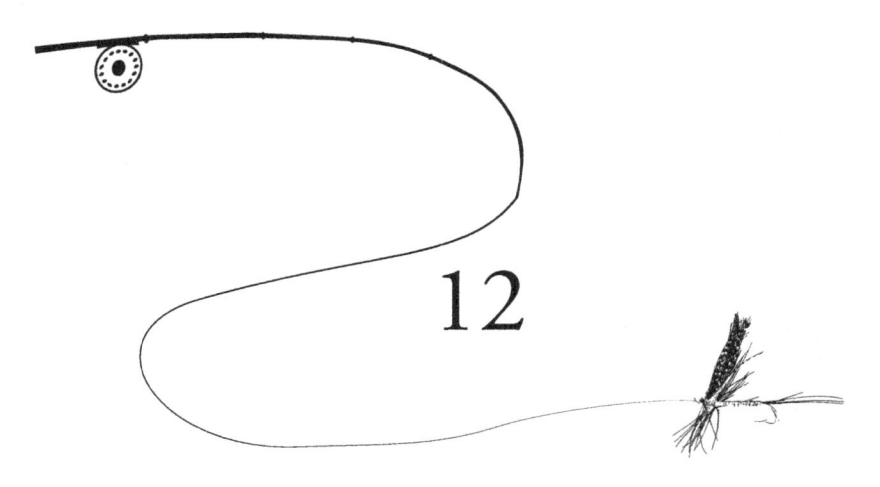

## Meeting Gail

Another day imprisoned in my room, another day tying flies. My stiff back tells me another evening is at hand. My eyes wander to the window and the growing shadows obscuring the Neversink. Whispering its leave, shy twilight ushers in a blustery dark, its wayward winds reminding me of Gail. Loneliness joins me, and I fondle her portrait. Raised in the remote north, Maine and the Adirondacks, a child of logging camps, leggings and Mackinaw coats, she swept me up to tramp the Catskills and to talk. Gail paid attention to me. Not the fly tier I am. Not the angler I am. But me. The man I am. Then she left for good. Gail confused me then, and her absence punishes me now. Day after day her intensity drove me. So often she said, "We're losing time." Long since parted from her, I now spend my days more leisurely.

A few years before moving to Liberty permanently, I was staying at Herron's Cottage on the Neversink. In those days I wandered the Catskills moving from boarding house to boarding house. It was June, mid-day, the heart of trout season, I was eating alone looking forward to an evening of fishing.

Gail and her mother paused at my table in the dining room. Nervous, her mother introduced herself, "Mrs. Walter Reynolds." Her clothes were fashionable but ill fitting; no dress maker's art could hide her muscular arms and shoulders and her scarred hands. I rose, bowed, and looked about to find two more chairs. Mrs. Reynolds interrupted my search, "No need. I will be brief." Gesturing to the black haired, young woman, standing stiffly beside her, she said formally, "I wish to introduce my daughter, Gail."

Taut with determination, Gail shot out her right hand. Her abruptness took me by surprise, and in reflex, I grasped it and bowed, "A pleasure Gail." Her mother frowned. I stared. Her eyes made me curious. Black, neither a warm black flecked with brown, nor a dull charcoal black, rather a lively black. A vital black.

Mrs. Reynolds asked if I was willing to teach her daughter fly fishing.

"For a fee," I replied.

When she asked my fee, Gail broke in, "Mother, we can afford it. Let's get to the point." Gail turned to me, "When can we meet for casting lessons?"

"Don't you want your mother to gather a few references before you entrust yourself to me?"

"I've never entrusted myself to any man," she replied. "In my father's logging camps, I learned to take care of myself, Mr. Theodore Gordon." Her mother flushed.

"Tomorrow at eleven on the porch."

It came in a rush and lasted for two years. That first day on the river Gail's mother dressed her up as a proper young lady vacationing in the mountains. Soft felt, forest green hat, woodland brown walking dress, and light green Turkish style drawers, all new. Herron's porch sitters nodded their approvals. She did not notice and ignored my compliments. Impatient to begin, she took my arm and skipped me down the hotel steps. Her pace was dizzying. In the lead, she dragged me scrambling down the banks of the Neversink just below Chandler's hotel to begin her first casting lesson.

A dry May lowered the river exposing its bouldered banks to a relentless sun firing them to a dull gray. She strode quick and sure over the rubble while I followed cautiously, more concerned with twisting an ankle than keeping up. Once Gail looked back questioningly which prompted me to pretend to check the fly rod. "A broken fly rod will end our session before it starts." It was then I became aware for the first time how my caution frustrated her. "Keep up!" She shouted over her shoulder.

Standing at the river's edge, waterproof camp shoes cinched tight, Gail began her lessons. I showed her the fly rod I brought for her lesson, a five and one quarter ounce Leonard split bamboo with a slim grip to fit her hand. She held it in front of her sighting down its length like it was a rifle. She switched it once, then bounced it up and down in her hand. "So light."

Gail was amazed at the thickness of the silk fly line. "You're casting the line, not the fly," I explained. She needed me to explain the purpose of the leader. My leader that day was seven foot of drawn gut. "The line nearest the fly must be invisible to the fish." The fly I attached was inconsequential because I did not expect to catch any fish. I removed the snelled fly from the line several times and then attached it slowly demonstrating how to loop it.

All in readiness, I flicked the line, leader and fly downstream into the current. By then we were standing shoulder to shoulder. And we had drawn a few onlookers. Watching the fly drift for a seconds minutes and then hang in the current, I flicked my wrist and made it sail upward and behind us. Then after a single beat count, I flicked it forward watching it settle again on the river. Only twenty feet of line and leader were out. "This is the basics," I said glancing over at her, "Now you try." Gail eagerly took the rod and swished it up and back without pausing. There was a snap and the line and fly fell limply at her feet. "You took the rod too far back and failed to count one beat on your back cast." She looked frustrated. "Try again. I'll make the count for you." The line swished back and hung for a beat and then straightened out on the forward cast. She turned with a quick smile, reward enough for me.

"Now we need to put out a little more line. This will test you," I explained. "With more line out the count goes a little longer," I said stripping ten more feet from the reel. Casting became impossible for her. The longer line demanded additional force to throw it up and behind. Gail misjudged the amount needed and forgot to make the count. More than strong enough, she heaved back too hard and then thrashed forward too soon. Again the rod went too far back and the fly line snapped again like a bull whip.

She handed the rod back to me, "It is not as easy as it looks." She was frustrated and her mood drove the onlookers away. I heard one say, "They aren't really fishing."

I took the rod from Gail and straightened out the line. "Watch closely and see what little effort it takes. Just the flick of a wrist."

Several more thrashings, I took the rod back and again straightened the line. "Go easy."

"I am making the count," she said.

"Yes, but you are trying too hard. Here, take the rod." She took the rod and I stood behind her, covering her casting hand with mine. "Now just feel the weight of the line. Sense its force and rhythm. You're casting the line, not the fly. Keep in touch with the line. It will tell you when to begin your forward cast." She relaxed and our hands together made perfect casts. We did this together a dozen times.

"Theodore Gordon, you have strong hands." Ignoring this remark, I released her hand. Afterwards she made one good cast for every two she tried. Swish…swish. Then I covered her hand again. And this time I sensed not only the line but I sensed Gail, her well-knit energy, her capable optimism, and her formidable reserve of energy to fully commit to whatever she chose.

Later returning to Herron's, I found a broom handle, cut it down and attached a length of string to it. "Practice tonight with this," I said offering it to her.

Refusing it, she retorted, "Practice it yourself. I'm taking lessons to meet you. I care little about fishing." Her mother flushed when

I glanced at her.

Again my eyes travel to her portrait, and I feel her hand in mine. And my loneliness deepens.

Fishing became our alibi for meeting. One day that first summer, we hiked upstream, well above the bridge in Bradley. Stopping at a stretch of the Neversink the locals called Big Bend, Gail put her arm through mine and, laughing, pulled me down on top of her. Quickly I rolled off and stood up, blushing.

"You're such a prude!"

"How old are you?"

"Old enough to know what I want."

"This is not what I want, young lady."

Patting the ground beside her, Gail said contritely, "Sit by me. I promise not to attack you." She smirked and tucked her hands between her legs. "Satisfied?"

Not knowing whether to laugh, I smiled vaguely. My attention was drawn to several decent sized trout rising along the edges of the pool. The sweeping curve of the river bounced up against a rock ledge setting off several small eddies. The circling currents caught and held small yellow flies. Noses of large brown trout engulfed them leisurely and then slid back.

"I'm more interesting than bugs."

"Maybe."

Gail stood up and stared into the river. "What are you looking at?"

"Yellow Sallies. They're floating on the edge of the current, and if you look hard, you will see them hovering just above the surface of the water farther out."

Just then a brook trout jumped and caught a Sally mid-air. "Wow." She looked over at me and said, "I'm still more interesting than bugs."

"Maybe."

"What are they doing?"

"Dropping eggs. They've just mated, and now they're dropping the fertilized eggs."

"Mated. So you do think about sex."

With that she took off her hat, shook out her thick, curly black hair and gave me a kiss. We did fish, and I made sure Gail caught a few. She dapped the edges. Quiet and careful, unmindful of the dust and mud, she crawled to the river's edge, a slinking cat. Lowering the line deftly so only the fly landed lightly on the water before circling freely, she looked over her shoulder. "This is how I fished worms up north." With whoops, she caught the best trout of the afternoon. We brought them back to Herron's for dinner. Afterwards, Gail's mother never questioned my lessons and our hours fishing together.

That summer there were more kisses. The following summer there were even more.

# 13

## The Bark Peelers' Stable

A year later, late summer, the Neversink ran low and clear. Nothing to show for the morning's fishing. On the bank, Gail sat draping an arm over our picnic basket. Dangling her bare feet in the river, impatient, bored, she challenged me to hike into the hills to eat lunch.

Reeling up my line, a letter from Marston praising his daughters came to mind and more to myself. I muttered, "I would like to have a daughter."

Gail heard. "Me too."

"A stray thought," I said faking disinterest. "How far up do you want to climb?"

"Have you given any thought to what you must do to have a daughter?"

"We should be looking for a path."

Gail laughed, "Theodore Gordon, we are going to have this conversation."

"Go ahead. It'll be a monologue."

Shading her eyes Gail searched the hillside. "Let's hike up to that clearing," she said pointing, "To that old log building."

Picnic basket and tackle in hand, I started the climb. Gail, excited, hurried on ahead. Reaching the clearing before me, she explored. Bark peelers felled a grove of hemlock not long before, built a small barn for their horses, and then abandoned it all. "You see how they worked?"

Naked tree trunks littered the hillside. Impatient for an answer, she went on, "They felled the hemlock across the slope. That way they could roll them down as they stripped off their bark with spuds. They started at the bottom of the grove and worked up. To save the horses." She stroked the bare wood. "Crosscut saws and axes mostly. An efficient crew."

Gail took the picnic basket and dropped it by the small barn. "Take a seat." Looking in through the door, she said, "There's still hay. Smells sweet. No broken chains. No forgotten wedges. A careful crew." The barn exhaled the smell of hay, and with it the reassuring smell of horses and sawn wood.

Gail sat opposite me and slid the picnic basket between us. "Now what were we talking about?" Forefinger to chin, looking into a pale sky, she blinked feigning forgetfulness. "We were talking. Yes, about something important wasn't it? Let me think… Let me think. Yes, about having a baby girl."

'No. That's not what we were talking about."

She grew thoughtful. "Again Theodore, you're right. We weren't talking about it. You were talking about it." I lifted the lid of the picnic basket and hunted in it for a new subject of discussion. Gail said curtly, "Tell me I'm wrong."

"You're not wrong." Pleading, I ventured, "I was thinking of Marston's daughters. An idle thought."

"An idle thought spoken to a young impressionable, unsophisticated woman of child bearing age. What am I to think?" I sighed in surrender and she, enjoying my discomfort, crooned sweetly, "Was that a proposal?"

"No."

"Are you leading me on?"

"No."

"Then let's be direct."

"With you there's no other way."

"Is my man of mystery complaining?"

"I don't like this conversation." I was about to say "young lady" but thought better of it. I had seen many relationships where the ages of the couple were as disparate as ours.

"I'd hoped you wouldn't." In a commanding voice, she started in, "Now I have few quick questions. And all I want from you are a few quick answers. One word answers. No stories. Do I have your attention?"

"Anything to end this absurd talk."

"Do you really want a daughter?"

"Yes." The answer came out without hesitation. It surprised me.

"Could you see having that daughter with me?" Uncomfortable, I dropped the lid of the basket. "Theodore, this is not hard. I am an attractive young woman. Some young men have even told me I'm beautiful."

"Yes." I said grudgingly.

"Let's be practical. Do you have what it takes to make a child?"

"This is too much." I said angrily. "Next you'll be asking for proof."

A smile played across Gail's lips. She rose, took me by the hand and led me into the barn. I followed knowing all the while I could have pulled away and walked back into the sun blanched clearing. I could have, but I did not. She held me in thrall.

I told myself that what we were about to do meant nothing and would change nothing. There would be no consummation of any understanding between us because there was no understanding between us. So I took off my coat and lay it on a pile of hay. A rustling of clothes, and she stood there naked, her undergarments a white hobble about her ankles. My mouth went dry and her beauty stopped what little breath I had. The pause shot a shiver of vulnerability through her. To dispel it, I offered my hand, and she stepped out of her hobble confidently.

And then we began. She, taut, summoning all of herself as was her way, to meet face to face what was to come. I, apprehensive, hanging back as was my way, afraid of what was to come. I remember her long, muscular legs binding me to her, my thrust of long dormant feelings, the searing agony of pent up pleasure, the wild eruption, and the helpless free fall into malaise. I lay panting, obliterated, as obliterated as I had lain on my many sick beds, after one more fevered crisis passed, after the shaking chills, after the consuming fire, all purpose wrung from me.

I was sadly right and sadly wrong. Right because that afternoon in the barn changed nothing between us. That was my doing. And wrong because that afternoon did mean something. For once in my life, I felt fully joined together with another person. And now without Gail I feel a more dreadful loneliness than I ever felt before.

Often at night before snuffing out my lamp, I finger Gail's portrait and see her laying back on the hay, smiling, lazily stretching an arm up into a shaft of sun light where golden chaff floated. She stirs them, and as they slow, they land softly, softly, shimmering gold dust flecking her arms, face and breasts. We slept, her golden arms entwined about me.

These many years later what has stayed with me is that Gail let me breathe on her. And then without flinching she let me kiss her. I still see my deadly saliva on her lips, glistening. Afterwards I feared for her life, and it was then I knew I loved her and would always love her. Even now, years later, I worry my consumption incubates in her lungs.

# 14

## Best Day, Best Year

Growing old brings few benefits. Most of them, on close inspection, are dubious. Vitality wanes and memory erodes. With each passing year, I fish less and less. Only when the trout are jumping do I venture forth. Even then, I lower my expectations. No longer strong enough to fish all day, I have subdivided my favorite stretches into shorter sallies, and so subdivided the number of my triumphs, my decline precisely measurable.

Reliving the past delivers more reliable results. It recalls the feel of my creel strap biting into my shoulder. No guesswork here, but then again, no anticipation here, no thrill here. The only game left is comparing old memories, one with another. And just as younger anglers confirm their fresh trophies by peeking into their creel again and again, so I reflect back, recounting again and again the stories of my best days.

My very best day occurred late July 1901. Its plot tracked so many plays Mother and I attended at the Savannah Theater. The day began in despair. Taking the train one afternoon to the Esopus above Phoenicia, I arrived just as a heavy rain washed out evening fishing. I thought of leaving, but no trains were running, so I stayed the night in a riverside inn. By morning, the creek had cleared somewhat, and though skeptical of success, I started fishing high, cold water in a dark overcast. Wading was difficult, and I was forced to make long casts to reach spots that held fish. I put on a nondescript fly, an experimental sparse tie. It had a yellow wool body on size 10 hook; the rest of the fly was washed in browns. The first fish of the day, a large brown trout, fell for the nondescript, and fought long and hard. During the fight, I guessed it went five pounds, but when I landed it, the trout came to only three.

More and more fish, some large, fell to the nondescript. Moments of challenge and risk punctuated the day. Gusting winds, difficult casts, brief drenching showers, vigorous tippet testing fights, and the daylong threatening storm clouds suppressed any feelings of elation. I will always remember the rain on the river that day, at moments hardly enough to imprint the surface, at others so explosive it churned the river to froth.

That day, despite the weather and the high water, I caught more than twenty-four fish, keeping twenty; many were of fair size and jumped during the fight. The numbers of fish and their size encouraged me, but the seesaw battles, the leaps of the big trout, and their powerful runs kept me on edge. It should be noted that my three-pound trout created a sensation back at the inn. With a catch of twenty-four trout, my day went well beyond what was a good day for Halford and any of his scientific anglers.

My best year fishing was 1906, the first year of my retirement from Wall Street. All summer, the Catskills' rivers ran full, clear, and cold. Mayfly and caddis appeared frequently and in great numbers. The trout fought well, running a pound heavier on average than any year before or since.

And I was healthy. Mother rode the O&W to Liberty after New Year's Day, and we took rooms together at the Liberty Hotel. That winter, her lungs gained strength quickly, thus relieving me of my nursing chores. Buoyed by Mother's return to health, we decided to take a cottage together June and July in the small village of Beaverkill. It was a momentous decision.

The cottage, white clapboard with green shutters, had four rooms. A better situation I could not imagine. A local woman cooked, cleaned, and was a companion to Mother. One room was set aside for fly tying, and the upper Beaverkill River flowed but a short walk away. The road fronting our cottage crossed the Beaverkill by way of a covered bridge. More often than not, my day began and ended at the bridge. For variety, some days I hopped a buggy south to the Willowemoc River. A few days I took the mail coach into the hamlet of Roscoe to fish the water below where the Beaverkill joined the Willowemoc.

Every day of the 1906 season stands out clearly in my memory. Several accounts are representative of the whole summer. One June day, I waded the big Beaverkill on water new to me. A long, broad, shallow rapids led to an equally long, but deep, pool. Most of the rapids was unremarkable except for a string of waist-high boulders guarding the north bank. In contrast, the pool was quiet with slow, obvious currents.

My fishing routine was simple. After casting quartering upstream, I kept my rod high, lifting up the slack forming as my fly floated down. Then after the fly passed, I slowly lowered the rod to mend and to feed out the slack so that the fly tumbled freely along the bottom dead drift. Once the slack was gone,

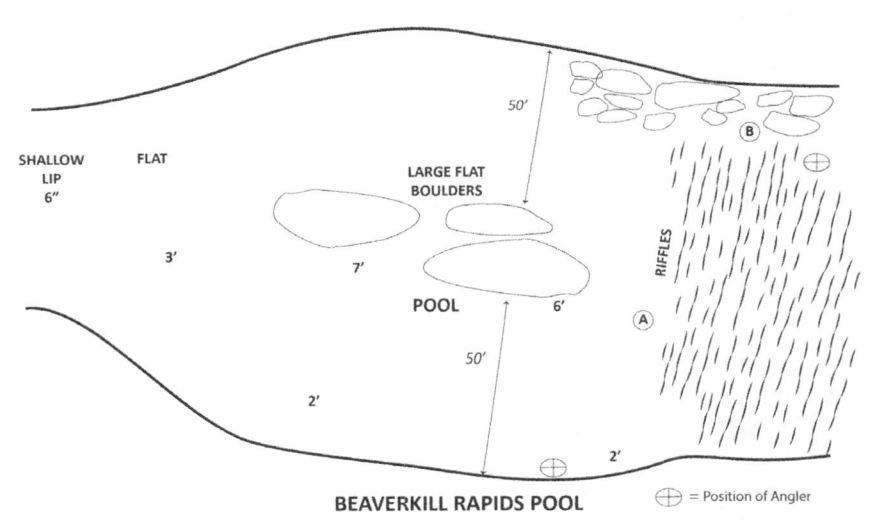

**BEAVERKILL RAPIDS POOL**    ⊕ = Position of Angler

the fly lifted and swung below me. It was monotonous work, which Habersham described as typical of salmon fishing. My reward:

four rainbows of a pound and a half each.

Approaching the point where the rapids dropped into the pool, I rang the colors. My fourth fly was on a #8 long shanked Black Gnat. At Point A, where the rapids entered the pool, a vicious strike caught me daydreaming. Twenty-five feet of line tore off my reel before I came to my senses. Fumbling, I snubbed the line to set the hook, but the fish did not slow. It took out another twenty-five feet of line before it jumped, a rainbow of good size. The fish and I raced each other downstream. It had a head start and lengthened its lead, for the bank was treacherous with loose rock and boulders, causing me to fall and bruise my knees at one point. Finally, when the fish slowed, shaking its head, I caught up and began retrieving line. The trout swung behind one of the flat boulders. I retrieved more line and began to worry the fish, keeping the line taut. The fish refused to move. So I waded just below it, maintaining a steady pressure.

The rainbow felt my presence. It slid from behind the boulder and charged into the main flow. Turning downstream with the strength of the river at its back, it ripped off another thirty feet of line. More running. The two of us reached the bottom of the pool together, exhausted. There the water shallowed up. Confused, the fish hesitated briefly in the shallow water, then shot back upstream a short distance, coming to rest on my side of the river. Retrieving more line, I saw it finning in a gravel depression. A tug forced it to slide back. It made no effort to regain the water it had lost. I tugged again, and it slid back farther. Ducking low, I edged up immediately below the fish and yanked my rod sideways, flipping it onto the bank. Flopping, trying for the river, it came to rest against a large rock, writhed once, and stilled. The big trout went four pounds. The smaller trout I gave to our cook. The four-pounder she baked with thyme, parsley, and butter. Mother was pleased.

A few days later, the same rapids witnessed another memorable scene. Still June, I was drawn to explore the boulders along the north bank. I found that the water among the boulders ran surprisingly slow and clear, with a scattering of three-foot holes.

Tying on a sparse, medium shaded Quill, I cast downstream to Point B, sliding my fly in and about the boulders. Several brown trout, one of two pounds, took it in creases between the boulders. They were of the dark variety.

Two miles upstream from the rapids sits one of the big Beaverkill's most mysterious waters. A moderate riffle of about a hundred yards leads into a picturesque pool. The riffle, split in two by a gravel bar, ran headlong into a rock face about twenty-five feet high and thirty feet long on the river's south bank. The rock face arrests all, stopping the riffle in its tracks, and deflecting it west. At the base of the rock face, a complex of currents churn for forty feet, eventually smoothing out to broaden into a shallow flat. The rock face is sheer and the south bank is precipitous.

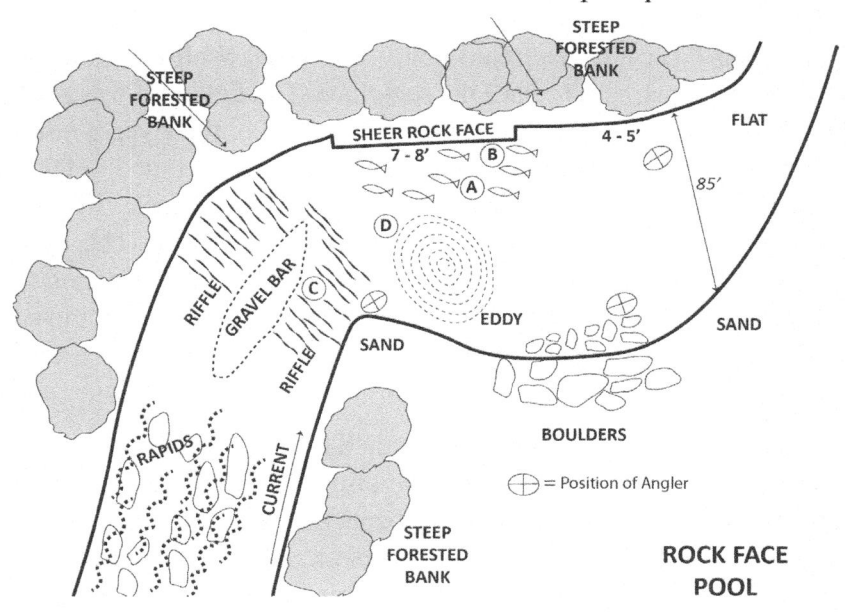

**ROCK FACE POOL**

The shadows cast by the rock face and the haunted, tangled, wild look of the nearby woods evoked the sublime. Its aspect commanded my interest. The pool held three strong markers of good trout water: a half-dozen mergansers nested on the north bank of the flats, a wizened Eagle perched high up a dead sycamore, and a bait fisher sat on the south bank, his pole supported by a forked stick.

On the north bank, a short, gently sloping path led to the pool. I took the path and arrived on the riverbank directly across from the rock face. Sitting on a boulder, I considered the scene. Large gray duns popped to the surface ten feet or so out from the rock face, and a line of trout formed, feeding on them. Wading out to Point A, I rang the colors without success. Returning to the boulder, I saw my lack of success was not a matter of the wrong color fly. Rather, the complex of currents and cross currents swirling before the rock face made a drag-free float near impossible. Nonetheless, I again challenged the currents, appealing to luck. Knotting on a longer tippet of one more x, I cast above the feeding trout, hoping for an accidental foot or two of dead drift. It never happened. Only one course of action was left, wading over to the south bank and fishing up from below.

Saluting the eagle, I circled below the pool. Well out into the flat, I waded upstream toward the rock face. The flat itself was knee deep, but, with each step closer to the rock face, the river bottom dropped until the water rose to chest high. Trout continued to feed. I selected a high floating, number 10 light Dark Cahill, checked my leader, and replaced the 2x tippet with a fresh one. The light Dark Cahill showed the light gray closest to the natural. Casting to Point B, I hit the pool's threads of current directly upstream and so achieved drag-free drifts. Some threads were no more than a foot wide.

Paying out more and more line, I made longer and longer casts. A slight breeze from the north pushed my casts closer to the south bank than I intended. One fell a dozen feet below the rock face about three feet out from its undercut bank. While considering the wisdom of picking my line up and making a more accurate cast, the fly disappeared in an emphatic rise. I struck and immediately felt the trout's power as it swung its tail to start its first run.

The fight was short. The fly lodged in the trout's jaw hinge, the scissors,and so prevented it from closing its mouth. Keeping the trout on a short line under maximum pressure, I saw it working its jaws. It was a large brown and lumbered about pointlessly, its mouth gaping. Impatient, I put my net in the water. Too soon. Once the trout saw the net, it backed off, weak, yet with enough power left for a few short runs. We battled back and forth. It took line, and I took it back. Another attempt to net the fish failed. Finally fighting for a few feet more of line, the net went into the water again. The fish shied but was now lying on its side. A beautiful brown trout of the yellow variety, large, better than four pounds. Mother and I shared it with our cook.

A few days later, I visited my mysterious pool again. Tired from long days fishing and my breathing labored from the climb down, I took a rest on the riverbank. Warmed by the sun, I fell asleep. Several hours later, a cool breeze woke me. I was alone. It was evening and the sun showed deep orange, its slanting rays already dimming. About an hour of light remained. The rock face was already lost in shadow. What I saw jolted me awake. Empty of anglers, the river was alive with mayflies, birds, and trout. Hundreds of duns filled the air. Blackbirds strutted the gravel bar, now reaching into the water to snag floating duns, now leaping up and snaring duns in flight. I waded knee deep into an eddy formed in a crook of the dogleg formed by the river bouncing off the rock face. The eddy was slow water, almost dead.

Pale yellow was the dominant color in the pool. Impatient, I looped on my first version of the Pale Evening Dun, a full hackled, high floater size #16. The light was sufficient to cast to individual fish feeding at Point C. None rose to my fly, although it passed over many. The pace of the hatch and my frustration accelerated. More casts to Point C and more refusals.

"Change flies, change flies." This time it was my third version of the Pale Evening Dun, again a full hackled, high floater, and again size #16. More casts, this time a few half-hearted strikes, but mostly refusals.

"Change flies; change flies. No!" Fighting off panic, I stopped and peered into fading light, doing what I should have done from the start. I fixed on the duns flapping aloft from the riffle. They ranged in size from #12 to #16. This time, I looped on a size right in the middle of the emerging naturals, a #14 of my fourth version Pale Evening Dun. But this time, instead of a high floater, I knotted on a sparse low floater. About a half hour of light was left before complete darkness fell, not enough time for another fly change.

No more casting to individual fish. Just blind casting to Point C in the riffle. Almost every cast brought a strike, and most strikes brought hookups. From the riffle came rainbows, hard fighters about a pound or two each. In all, five came to hand and were quickly slipped into my creel. Another two were on briefly but jumped and were lost. The light was almost gone, and the shadows falling off the steep upland along the south bank obscured the river's surface. The emergence slackened and fewer rises showed in the riffle. As the sun's rays rose, slowly lifting off the surface of the pool, a plane of orange light hung suspended in mid-air for a moment. And in that plane, I saw other species of mayflies flapping upward. They were large and gray. Of that I am certain.

No time to change flies again, so I continued casting the #14 Pale Evening Dun. In the dark, I heard, rather than saw, desultory rises in the slow eddy in front of me. I cast to the closest edge of the riffle, Point D, and felt the line swing as the fly entered the eddy. Guessing the risers in the eddy were cruising for cripples and drowned duns, I gently pulled my fly under and twitched it slightly a time or two. A strong strike, a fight, and a glistening brown of the dark variety, about two pounds, came to hand. Another cast and another fish. This happened three more times. By then, profound night had engulfed the pool. I was worried about the climb back up to the road and the long walk home in the dark. So I left.

That evening, the Beaverkill showed a generous face demanding thoughtful consideration. As a friendly host, it took me in and offered a great banquet if I could answer its one question, "What fly?" It was patient with me and gave me three tries.

The next evening, I went back to my mysterious pool, looking for a repeat of the previous night's action. I was ready with the effective fly. A bait fisher and a fly fisher beat me there. The bait fisher again claimed his spot on the south bank. The fly fisher stood in the quiet eddy where I had stood the previous evening. I sat and watched, waiting. Nothing happened. The fly fisher and the bait fisher left troutless. I waited some more. Still nothing. Not a single mayfly fluttered up from the riffle, and no rises sounded in the dead water. Out of the dark, I believe I heard a scornful laugh, another face of the Beaverkill.

The following winter, 1907, Mother was very ill and needed intensive nursing. Some days she could hardly dress or feed herself. In spring, she returned healthy to South Orange. By then, from the worry and long hours of nursing her, my health suffered, and I was too exhausted to fish or tie flies for the greater part of the 1907 trout season.

After 1906, drought and flood cycled more frequently. The spring floods filled the deep holes with debris, and the rivers ran shallower and warmer by July. Now all the spring floods do is shift the debris. Our rivers have lost their character, pools become flats, and by August, riffles become stagnant puddles. In the very dry years, the big trout are either poached or frightened down to the Delaware.

## 15

## Interview with Gail's Father

Up to her knees in the Neversink, Gail stood changing flies. Her loose black hair glistened in the bright sun as she squinted to thread her leader through a hook's eye. Lighthearted, Gail hummed:

*Daisy, Daisy, give your answer, do.*

*I'm half-crazy all for the love of you.*

*It won't be a stylish marriage....*

Fly knotted on, she flipped it out, announcing, "Father came up by train last night. He wants to interview you."

"For what?"

"Theodore, we've spent two summers together. We love each other. I know it. You know it even though you won't talk about it. It's time we think about something more permanent."

"Like marriage?"

"Thank you for proposing." She looked over her shoulder as she cast, "If my father approves, you may have my hand in marriage."

It was useless to argue, "I doubt if your father has much say in the matter."

"He has none."

"So why the charade?"

"He demands decorum, and decorum requires a suitor ask his blessing before proposing to his daughter."

"So all I need do is act out the charade."

'If you wouldn't mind. Father will say "yes" because he knows no man would dare ask for my hand if I didn't put him up to it.'

For weeks a crisis had been building. Tired of the Catskills, Gail fantasized about wilder, emptier places. The thought frightened me. I wanted to go on as we had, an endless summer of picnicking and fishing, the clink and clatter of silverware and stemware, the pleasant aromas of hotel dining rooms, baked pies, roasts, salvers of sweet gherkins, the click and slap of new leather soles on waxed hardwood floors, shadowed porches and iced lemonade in the midday heat, the cool of ironed sheets at night. I felt no need to seek adventure. I was happy with our routines and dreaded the thought of traveling to places without a uniformed wait staff.

To observers, Gail acted the engrossed angler anxious to be off in the morning. They did not see her as I did, the days wading secluded sunlit pools, all lovers drawn to her. There was the day, surrounded by willows, arms outstretched, she stood wrapped in damsel flies, dozens quivering emerald and sooty gray on her hat and shoulders. Moving stiffly, casting tentatively, talking quietly, prolonging the grace of their company, love's beacon, Gail cooed to them as they sat, smoky wings folded back, awaiting the call to intercourse. And then too long constrained, laughing, she clapped her hands and scattered the throng, with a "Shoo!"

In the whites of Herron's dining room with its starched tablecloths and bustle, Gail's father stood out. He arrived before me, more than punctual, sipping coffee, halfway through the morning's *New York Herald*. A beige three piece linen suit, gold watch chain, and dark blue tie distinguished him, all business in this land of straw boaters and leisured table talk. He was easily two of me and dwarfed all the breakfasting patrons. I expected the lumberman who worked his way up from land looker to land owner, once fit now grown flabby as he spent more time in the office with lawyers, engineers, and accountants. Instead he sat, a strong, lean man whom I could imagine on a bet taking off his coat and swinging an ax racing the best of his crews to the crack and swish of a dropping pine. He stood up and gestured toward a chair.

I extended my hand, "Theodore Gordon, sir. Sorry I'm late."

'You're not late. I still hear the cry, "Daylight in the Swamp" at first light, an old habit I can't shake." He offered a tanned hand, muscled with scarred knuckles. "Walter Reynolds. Walt is fine." He inspected me, "If you don't mind, I'll call you Ted. We're close enough in age to be on a first name basis." We sat, he barely contained by his chair which creaked when he shifted.

"Ted will be fine, Walt." It was not fine. The formalities of "sirs" and last names kept a polite distance. That distance slowed conversation giving me time to compose elegant, lengthy answers, more entertaining and suggestive than factual. I promised Gail I would take this interview seriously. It called for the largest empty canvas on which to paint my legend in broad strokes. "Ted" held me to jottings.

Mr. Reynolds sensed my reluctance, turned away, sipped his coffee and plunged in ignoring my discomfort. "Ted, have you done any book keeping?" He asked.

Dismayed, I looked up questioningly. "Book keeping?"

"Yes. Book keeping. You know debits and credits, assets, balances?"

His directness demanded directness. Little time for consideration, I gave succinct, mostly accurate answers. "Of course. Yes, I've worked part time as a book keeper for a Savannah bank just before coming back north. Also I balanced my uncle's books. He owns a Wall Street firm. Complicated transactions involving every type of property, losses and gains and such."

"That's helpful. What management experience have you had?"

"I managed my own brokerage firm in Savannah. It was

profitable...until the Panic." I hesitated, quizzical again.

Sensing my mounting confusion, Mr. Reynolds explained, "You have no idea what I'm talking about do you?"

"No."

"Gail asked me to interview you for a job. I need trustworthy people in Menominee, a fledgling Michigan city overrun with loggers and logging operations. I'm spending more of my time West and need someone to take over the Menominee office. You and Gail would fit the bill."

"I thought you wanted to question me about...."

Mr. Reynolds held up a hand to stop me. "By now you know Gail, Ted. She's always two steps ahead of everyone around her, including me. She says you'll need a job when you two are married."

"I have a small salary from my Uncle's Wall Street firm, some income from a mail order tackle business, and a few investments."

"According to Gail all too small to raise a family," His black eyes, so like Gail's, wandered the room and then returned to me, "This Menominee job she thinks perfect for you. I'm partners with Judge Stevens; he runs the town. We went in together, you know, forest tracts, lumber mills, railroads, engineers, crews...everything. We chute the trees down the Brule and Paint rivers, boom them in Menominee and Marinette, and turn them into finished boards right there. We ship all over the Great Lakes. A good business. Should go another twenty years."

"I did not expect this." The gush of information left me breathless.

"Gail is always in the middle of the unexpected. Think about the job. It would make her happy if you took it. And if it's not too much to ask, I'd like your answer before the family and I catch the train back to Manhattan tomorrow. If it's a yes, you're welcome to come with us."

"This is rather sudden." Nostalgic for her early days growing up in her father's logging camps, Gail talked about going west, back to the demanding life she knew in the woods.

"If it makes you feel any better, I can ask you future son-in-law questions. Let's see." He took another sip of coffee, "Do you own any real estate?"

"No."

"Not even a house?"

"No." He showed surprise.

"Any investments? You know stocks and bonds."

"Some and most of the income goes to my mother. She's an invalid."

"So you really have nothing."

"Nothing but my writing and fly tying business."

"No matter. You're well-mannered, and from what I've heard from Gail, smart too. You'll fatten your bank account in Menominee." As an afterthought, he added, "We'll get along fine," smiling broadly as he said the words.

"I'm sure we will."

"Ted, you must realize that marriage is just a legal formality to Gail, something which must be done before you two can live together respectably. It means no more to her than filling out a passport application before traveling overseas. It's the living together with you she wants, not the wedding, not the ring. She wants a family."

Mr. Reynolds paused and then coming to a decision pressed on. "You're the man she's settled on so I'm in favor of you. The Menominee job is yours if you want it. You and Gail will be in charge of the office when I'm away, which is most weeks. I've been traveling northwest looking to buy new forest properties. Washington, Oregon, Montana, Idaho, you know. Nailed a few down." His voice was triumphant. "Gail knows the business so if anything complicated comes up while I'm gone, she'll know what to do."

"I'm hungry." Mr. Reynolds signaled the waitress, "We're ready to order."

"A few eggs and toast. More tea, if you have time," I said holding my cup up.

"Do you have pancakes?"

"Yes, sir."

"Then pancakes it is." Looking over, Mr. Reynolds said, "I've never found any breakfast better than what our camp cooks turned out. My wife and Gail were the best of them."

"Gail misses those days."

"It was a good time for our family. A bit risky at the start; we lived poor, but we saved money and had some luck. Put everything we saved back in the business. You're fortunate, spending money makes Gail uncomfortable. She's just like her mother."

"Gail's often told me there's nothing so heady as waking up in a logging camp in the dead of winter."

Mr. Reynolds sat back summoning memories of being married with a young wife and daughter, living in rude log buildings far from the nearest towns. "Everything that can happen in life will happen sooner or later in the woods. The cold shocking you awake in the morning; the frozen fingers and clumsy minutes starting a fire; the fire's cheery reds and oranges, the creeping warmth; the glowing stoves, the smell of wood smoke, bacon sizzling, griddles covered in eggs and pancakes; the men clumping into the cook shanty, their low murmurs, the occasional laugh, thankful for a half hour of heat and all the food they can eat before picking up their axes and saws and heading into the snow. On the coldest days, Gail and her mother brought coffee and sandwiches to the crews. There's nothing like the smell of fresh cut wood and coffee in the still of a forest morning, the snow mantling all."

"Don't get me wrong. There were bad days too. Death was all about us. We were all at risk. Runaway skidders crushed men on icy roads. Felled trees dropping off-line crushed others. Widow makers invisible in top branches pierced lumberjacks working below. And then there were the deaths on the rivers, men who lost their footing while walking the logs, men who slipped under jams while setting dynamite charges, so many young men. Imminent death made us realize the worth of each one of us. We needed each other. We depended on each other. Not just Gail, her mother and me, but the whole crew. It's a special feeling that I miss when I'm away from the woods too long." There was a pause, and I thought Mr. Reynolds was done, when he said gently, "Gail misses that feeling too. Even her finishing schools couldn't shame that out of her."

Mr. Reynolds gestured as he spoke. He moved as few large men I knew moved, all of a piece. When gesturing, all his muscles synchronized as tied to a single thought, always efficient, never overly dramatic. That morning in Herron's dining room I understood the reason. Logging fostered careful movement, the sort of movement which does not call down risk.

"That's why Gail is so different from other women. She's lived poor and seen death. Her mother and I didn't shield her from the ugliness of life. And we did not tell her fairy tales to help her sleep through the night."

Mr. Reynolds looked over at me. My turn to say something, and all I could say was the truth, "She's extraordinary." Mr. Reynolds smiled. He knew the truth when he heard it.

Our breakfasts arrived with fresh pots of coffee and tea. I picked at my food while Mr. Reynolds ate quickly. Between bites, he said, "From what Gail tells me, you disapprove of logging."

Surprised at myself, I replied immediately, "Yes, it's ruined the Catskills. While the rivers you see about you are beautiful and a joy to fish for a few months in the spring and early summer, they struggle with ice dams in the winter, eroded banks during spring freshets and heavy rains, drought and low water in late summer and sawdust covered spawning beds in the fall. All due to hillsides scalped clean of all trees. Their only hope for recovery is a stop to all logging. I dread the future of what were, before the mills and the clear cuts, the most prolific trout rivers in this country."

Mr. Reynolds grew thoughtful. "Then you'd have a problem working for any logging company following similar practices?"

"Yes. I'll only work jobs I can square with keeping rivers as they were before logging."

Mr. Reynolds sat back smiling, "Ted, you and I think more alike than you know. You've heard of Gifford Pinchot?"

"Yes."

"He and I are friends. Following his advice I've sent one of my bright young lumberjacks to his Yale School of Forestry. Next year when he graduates, he'll return and help me modernize our operations. I'm sold on conservation. You've probably read the essays by Pinchot and his friend Teddy Roosevelt."

I nodded, "The editor of *Forest and Stream*, George Grinnell allies himself with Roosevelt and Pinchot. I follow Grinnell's editorials and where I can, I support his policies. I'm indebted to him for buying my fishing articles. Most sportsmen support Grinnell's vision. Reforestation will stabilize riverbanks, end flooding, and cool the rivers. Thus going into the future, our rivers will hold more fish. It's a simple cure. And its simplicity makes for a powerful argument."

"We're closer than you think," Mr. Reynolds said, becoming animated. "My company will be the first to apply conservation principles to forestry practices. If you worked for me, you could help bring this about. Together we could save hundreds of rivers from the fate your Catskill rivers suffered." He paused, as if searching for the right words, then when he had them, started tentatively, "Gail tells me you have a gift for writing. You could write articles about what my company's doing and convince more lumbermen to adopt a conservation ethic."

With the new job came a cause. I was hesitant to enlist, "I would not think conservation would bring you any profit." conservation do for you?"

Mr. Reynolds noted the evasion. Subdued he began, "I can stop moving west every few years. We've been reseeding pine plantations from Maine to Michigan. When those trees mature, we'll harvest and reseed again. It will take a while I know, but there'll be no need to invest in new land, set up new camps and hire new crew. We'll become managers of forest lands rather than gypsies. In the long run it'll be more profitable, and I'll leave my family a going business."

The idea of writing advertising copy for a lumber company, even one that practiced conservation, appalled me. No longer listening closely, I stiffened and drew back, "Let me talk to Gail about it." I wanted Gail, not a cause.

Sales pitch rebuffed, Mr. Reynolds frowned. Disappointment played across his face. Recovering momentarily, he laughed, "Remember Ted, whether you join my company or not, all I ask of you and Gail is to live respectably. That's all I've wanted for her. I believe you understand that."

"Of course, Walt. I want that too."

Mr. Reynolds smiled, sat back, and laid his knife and fork on his empty plate.

Taking another sip of coffee, he stood up, "Excuse me, please, I must look in on Mrs. Reynolds. We've planned a day together." Another glance and another smile. Mr. Reynolds believed in the long game.

# 16

## Parting

Evening, alone, half way through a glass of Madeira, my mind slows and quiets. A few kernels of corn tossed to my noble friend. Thwack, thwack. A welter of memories crowd in. I roll a cigarette before posing the question, "Which one shall I savor first?"

A memory. Late January, days in the high 30's, nights in the 20's, thawing and freezing, the snows about Bradley glazed over. Having a taste for roast grouse, I wandered the glare with my Parker. Skirting the Neversink's uneven, icy banks, I skated the edges of farm fields. Tan corn leaves fluttered from dried stalks like guidons marking the tangle of fence post, vine and cane roofing grouse burrows. I kicked them in and in the clamor rising from my boots shot three. Jennie roasted them pinned with bacon and served them with a sugar plum sauce.

Another sip of Madeira...another memory. Mid-July, a rocky pool on the Neversink, sitting, waiting for a legendary great brown trout to feed. The third evening of my vigil. A dribbling hatch of large cream colored mayflies pulls up a few fish. Rise rings cover the pool. I wait. More mayflies appear. Then a quiver of black separates from an underwater ledge and swims deliberately to the head of the pool scattering a half dozen smaller fish. The legendary trout. Mayflies pass over it. And it starts feeding.

My kit bag and sure fingers create the fraud. The fish commands thin water, water requiring delicate casting. The leader point I choose balances delicacy and the fish's great weight, light enough not to raise its suspicion yet heavy enough to turn it when it charges downstream to the heavy rapids below.

More patient observation. The trout does not sip naturals singly. It opens its mouth and with its upper jaw above the surface scoops in three and four at a time. There is a rhythm to it. Feeling the tempo, I breathe evenly and, so calmed, cast to the fish's beat. The fly settles softly in a cluster of mayflies. The trout's jaw breaks the surface and on beat inhales the cluster. My strike startles it into a leap. I see its sides streaming water, dark brown and yellow, more than two feet long; I see the leader across its jaws; I see its sharp teeth clamp down; and I feel the line go slack.

Day by day, with its escape, the legend of the trout grew in the neighborhood. And as with all legends, not of our species, yet surviving within our midst, the great fish became an affront to humankind. One night not long after my encounter, a posse formed under cover of darkness. As the great fish rested secure in its prowess, the posse seined its stronghold stampeding the legend into their net where they killed it for its arrogance. My fly was still stuck in its mouth. It went over six pounds. They brought me its head.

Another sip of Madeira...Herron's. My interview with Gail's father over, I find Gail in a rocking chair on the front porch. She jumps up, "What took you so long?" as the front screen door clapped behind me.

Today Gail's impatience is annoying.

She sensed it, "You've made up your mind against the job, haven't you? I can read it on your face."

I lied, "No, I haven't. I don't know what to think. The Menominee job is overwhelming."

My reluctance frustrated her. "It's really very simple. If we go west, we've a future together. If we don't, we have none."

"I find it hard to leave my life here."

"What holds you? It can't be your mother. We'll make enough to pay for her care, and she can visit us summers."

To reassure Gail, I said hurriedly, "No, no, it's not mother. Let me say before you start in that I do admire your father very much."

Gail took my arm and skipped me down the front steps. Together we turned into the road running along the Neversink. Before she could speak, I started, "Please Gail, I need to think this through by myself."

Ignoring me, she said, "Let's talk seriously about our future. I'll go first."

"I'm in no mood for your unvarnished truth."

"It's the only one I know." She glanced over at me severely. I glared straight ahead to show my displeasure. 'So let me begin, Theodore. You're what people call a hanger-on. You've the manners and speech practiced by the wealthy but not their bank accounts. You're faking who you are to get close to the wealthy men you serve. When your mask slips, and it slips often enough, the wealthy see through you. I flush with shame, when you're found out.

"Stop right there, Gail. I set my own course," and then added firmly, "I haven't done so badly up to now."

She turned, pity coloring her face, 'I could tell you as your wealthy friends might, "You're trying to live above your station." But that would be unfair, for I see what your customers don't see. I see your talent. I see the man you could be.'

Quickly, I shot back, "I am content with my salary, writing and fly tying business."

"Are you telling me you want nothing more for the rest of your life than the pittance you receive? It will not support a family."

"It's regular." A pause and an afterthought, "What else is left me?"

"Theodore, don't start in about your consumption. If anything, your consumption's makes you interesting."

Surprised, I blurted out, "You can't be serious."

"I am. Your consumption turned you into a writer, and a very good writer at that."

"I started writing to advertise my name."

"No matter your purpose. What you don't realize is that along the way you developed an engaging literary style. Your many readers feel the same way, I'm sure. I see a future where you write popular books about little known western waters. Adventure stories. Next summer we could boat Lake Superior as Robert Roosevelt did and fish the North Shore. The Nipigon River is worth a trip. Material enough for a first book. It's a short lake steamer ride from Menominee."

Cornered I said, "Let me tell you what I see." Turning towards her my eyes narrowed with anger, "I see myself doing exactly what I'm doing right now. It's taken me years of work to get to this point. I've a small business with satisfied customers, and I've editors who publish my articles. I'm not going to throw that away and start all over again at my age."

"If we go west together, you could remake yourself…become what you've always wanted to be. Don't you see everybody here is sorted out? You've been assigned your place and that is where you'll remain as long as you stay here."

We were at an impasse. Irritated, I said, "Here I have found out who I am. There are days I'm the best angler in the Catskills, and on those days, I don't mind being thought of as a hanger-on. Out west, I've no idea what I'd become. Let's say you're right, and I do write books. Perhaps my books won't sell. And if they don't, people will still think me a hanger-on, an old man living off his rich, young wife."

"Out west you'll become whatever you make of yourself. That's all anyone can ask of this life…a true measure of your worth. It's my belief you'll become a great writer." Then Gail looked fiercely into my eyes and said, "I have faith in you. We will make a great team. Your strengths will make up for my weaknesses. You're well mannered, well spoken, discreet, and more importantly you have the patience to keep records. I have none of your gifts. And need I repeat myself and remind you of your writing ability. I want our children to inherit your gifts."

"I've seen defeat, Gail, pursuing big dreams," I replied. "It's very possible if I leave here, I'll be leaving my best days behind. Going west could be my final step down into failure. I'd be giving it all up to chase an unrealistic dream, and not even my dream, your dream."

Gail did not flinch. "Not my dream! It's you who wants to write a book about fishing. Do it!"

"I haven't time. You know that. All I can realistically hope for now are more customers for my flies and time to write my essays. The people I want to impress fish here in the Catskills, and that is why they read my articles."

"Your good days here mean little to your wealthy customers. While you're thinking how much better a fisherman you are, they're thinking of buying the perfect stretch of river, the best waders, the finest rods and reels, things you can't afford. And when they've laid out the money, they believe they've bested you."

Stung, I raised my voice, "You're too young to understand. In their thoughtful moments, they respect me for being the better fisherman."

"No, Theodore, I've lived with these people. I've been to their schools and drunk tea in their drawing rooms. It makes no difference how many big brown trout you catch while they're catching brook trout hardly days out of the hatchery. You think you've beaten them. Not so. Your success simply prods them to spend more money. To their mind they win when they compare their expensive rods and reels to your cheap ones. They win when they reminisce about their trips to England's chalk streams and

Canada's salmon rivers. Trips you cannot afford. They win when in the evening they sit around the best hotel common rooms sipping whiskey with others of their society while you chat in farmhouse kitchens over coffee with the likes of Roy and Christian."

Angry, tempted to walk off, I stepped back from her. Sensing my upset, Gail reached out a hand and lightly grasped my arm, "I take no pleasure in what I'm saying. I'm fighting for a new future for us, a clean slate, married away from here."

"You're wrong. These people seek out my advice; they praise my articles. I'm known here."

"You're an ornament here, just one of a legion of writers and artists who flock to the Catskills, lending it some color. That's all."

"Is this what our married life will be like? You, nagging me to make something of myself."

Bowing her head, Gail said quietly, "I'm sorry you feel that way. But you're shutting me out of an important decision, one which affects the two of us. That's hard for me to accept."

"I need some time alone."

Gail stepped in front of me and put a hand on my chest. "I can help. Why not tell me what you're thinking? We can go through it point by point. If in the end you decide to stay, at least I'll know why."

"No. Right now I'm too upset to know what I think."

"Theodore, married and west, every day will be a new adventure. You have the genius of originality. Feed it with new rivers and new country. With me. You'll see. We'll make a great team."

"I'll never become the man you want me to be. I'm too old and the time is not far off when you'll lose interest and discard me." Sadness born of pessimism stood palpably between us. It was the sadness of caution, of being adrift among bright prospects without an appetite for change.

Troubled Gail said, "Do me one favor. Consult your heart."

Then making as to go she half turned and said, "We'll be at the Liberty House tonight having supper."

"Once I've considered everything, I'll join you there." An evasion. My heart told me to go west with Gail. What my heart could not tell me was whether striking out anew I could make a success of it. If I failed, I would be forced to rely on Gail and a salary from her father's lumber company for support. It was the same fear I felt leaving Savannah, the fear of being at another's beck and call, the fear of losing my independence.

Perceiving the evasion, Gail refused to give up. "Is there anything I can say which will help you think this through?"

"No."

"I know you quite well, Theodore. And as with so many, you fear falling into poverty. That fear is worse than poverty itself. The fact is you've never been poor." Fixing me with her black eyes, agitated now by my evasions, Gail repeatedly poked me in the chest with one of her slender fingers, "Theodore, I know poverty, and I can say it's liberating. It tells you what's important in life, and it tells you who your real friends are. You've known neither and staying here you've no chance of ever finding out."

Rocked by her words, I stood speechless. Into the silence, Gail spat out, "If Menominee doesn't work out, I'll be back next summer. And if you're more open with me then, we'll pick up where we left off. If Menominee does work out, I'll not be back."

"If that's what you want..." Gail had challenged my deepest fears and forced me to choose. Losing what little I had and living catch as catch can on the frontier frightened me.

"It's not what I want. It's all you're allowing me. You should learn to believe in your considerable talents. With or without me." Gail leaned forward and kissed me. "Take care. I hope to see you at the Liberty House."

Restrained, I kissed her lightly on the cheek. Disappointed, she looked at me when we broke our embrace, and I could tell she doubted I would be joining her and her family for supper that evening. The crisis was upon us, and I did what I have done so often, I sought distance from it. Turning away, I said, "Just give me a few hours."

Plaintively, she cried, "I don't know what else to say." Quickly she ducked her head. With two swipes of the back of her hand, she looked up, angry, her face streaked with tears, walking backwards in the dusty road, "Theodore, to become your own person, you must risk yourself, testing yourself against your dreams, pushing yourself every day no matter how low you feel. Otherwise you'll become a narrow man planning a narrower future. Don't become that man." Then she turned and strode head high, determined into my past.

That afternoon, alone, I let my mind run. It dove into my deepest self and found only doubts, and with each doubt my mind pulled up the fear which spawned them. So hours later I returned to Herron's beset with an army of doubts and fears. Sweaty, shoes dusty, tired, I inquired at the front desk whether Gail and her parents were in. "No. They've been out all evening, Mr. Gordon." Relieved I went up to my room and hid. There is no other word for it. I hid. I hid from Gail's unvarnished truths. I hid from confronting her again.

Next morning, sleepless, watching dawn creep across the ceiling of my room, I lay in bed confused. How could I tell Marston and Skues I was moving to the frontier? Would my relationship with the *Gazette* end and the interest of its readers dry up? *Forest and Stream* would still welcome my articles and there were always *Outing* and *Outdoor Life*. Maybe. What would the members of the Anglers' Club and the Fly Fishers say? Would they laugh snidely at the scandal of me, a middle aged man, taking a child bride? Would they say my passions for some silly young girl had addled my brain? Or that I was throwing away my notoriety on the rude daughter of some *nouveau riche* lumberjack. After a sleepless night, with my room bathed in soft morning light, I faced my real doubts. Would I fail as an author? Would I become a kept man?

Sophistry won out. I decided not to decide. And I felt good about my indecision because for the moment my independence remained intact. If I could not make up my mind, I was better off going on as I had always gone on. Alone. A free agent. What I should have done but did not do was recall my last conversation with Neyle and examine my deep need for independence. As he suggested, that need was perhaps my greatest flaw.

Staying in my room all morning, I put off venturing downstairs until Gail and her parents left for the depot. My cowardice imprisoned me. Late morning looking out my window, I saw her and her mother and father walking down Herron's front steps to a waiting carriage. Mr. Reynolds spoke quickly in low tones as he handed Gail up to her seat. As she mounted the carriage, Gail turned and looked up at the windows to my room. Before I could jump behind the curtains, she saw my terrified face. Following her eyes, Mr. Reynolds saw my curtains falling back. Angrily he shrugged and said something to Mrs. Reynolds who put an arm around Gail's slumped shoulders.

As the carriage pulled away, the driver slapped the reins on the team's backs. The report marked off that irretrievable moment between my life with Gail and my life without her. In that moment, I could have run downstairs and shouted for her to wait. I could have borrowed a horse and raced to join her at the station. That moment stood there, real, before me. And I shrunk from it. So that moment passed forever and with it my chance for a family with Gail.

Not long afterwards, my loneliness returned ever more painful. I saw clearly that refusing to make a change changes everything. It changes how you look on your whole life afterwards. And this remains true whether you keep on doing what you have been doing or not. Deciding against a future with Gail revealed me for the man I am. And every day since I face the present moment, as I faced the moment Gail's carriage drove away. I face it as a coward.

That next spring I took noon meals at Herron's lingering in the dining room, slowly drinking tea, expectant, waiting. When she did not appear, I wrote her. My letters came back unopened, "addressee unknown". Facing the obvious, I thought of inquiring of her forwarding address, but reconsidered and did not. It was rumored I had been disappointed in love. I was afraid voicing my curiosity would prove the rumor. Too painful a concession to the gossips.

Gail never returned to the Catskills. Without inquiry, I let her go. Far better to treat her departure as one more fishless day or the slight tug of an empty game bag on my shoulder, my dignity intact, confident my luck would change, yet knowing all the while it would not. Once she showed me the trail head, but when I dithered, she stepped off into the frontier on her own, never to return. Even now I see her ahead of me. She stops and half turns, smiling, morning sunlight shining behind her, as she beckons me to step into her future, a future of new horizons. Instead I cling to my secrets, too heavy a burden to pack into her wilderness. So now I shuffle slowly into my future, constrained by loneliness. Bitterly uneasy about what is to come.

Yes, not going with Gail changed everything. If I had ridden with her to the station discussing our wedding date, she would be lying beside me now instead of her picture.

# 17

## Trophy Brown Trout

New York State stocks Catskill rivers with both brook and brown trout. Many brown trout hold over, surviving from one year to the next. If it were not for brown trout, the lower stretches of most Catskill rivers would be bass and chubb water. Few brook trout hold over. It is not their lack of sophistication that makes them vulnerable; it is their need for cold water. Late summer droughts do them in. They crowd springs and run up cold feeder creeks. As they starve, anglers feast on them. The fishing, they say, is "Just like the old days."

Preparing for trout season, I am reminded of President Roosevelt's charge to engage fully in the strenuous life. For me, the strenuous life is fishing for old brown trout in public water. They demand the most of the fly fisher, and so are the truest test of an angler's worth.

The abstemious brown trout survive. Feeding in impossible places at impossible times, they have the discipline to pass on any tasty-looking item that does not strictly obey the laws of gravity and inertia. They stakeout lies in deep water in the midst of complex currents born of snags, boulders, and tree roots. Meticulously studying their several square yards of river, they become expert in the movement of natural food through their lair. They could write the definitive book on dead drift and the effects of upwellings on tumbling nymphs, minnows, and worms.

Old brown trout hear all, remember all. They mark every note struck by their river. For years, they store up the chatter of riffles, the sizzle of whipping currents sliding along gravel bars, and the roar of leaping waves crashing down on boulders. When the river melodies change, they flee. It may be the splash of an angler stepping into the river. Or it may be the grinding of gravel as an angler shift his or her weight, distracted, picking through a fly box. So, too, they associate the angler's alien presence with flashes of light reflecting off varnished fly rods, waving white hands, and polished aluminum fly box lids. They are suspicious of silt clouds, interpreting them like warning smoke signals. They know the difference between a clumsy wading angler and a deer planting its front feet in the water before taking a drink.

Public waters sort out the very smartest brown trout from their weak-minded brothers and sisters. Catskill brown trout in public water have seen every bait, fly, and lure humans have devised. And despite the odds, some survive for many years, never feeding on whim, never feeding out of curiosity. True to their calling, careful and suspicious, they are more patient than any angler. They are the fittest of their species, their virtue reproof to the mediocre. Trout that swim unmolested for months in private water cannot confer the mantle of expertise on any angler. Only smart brown trout surviving in public waters can do that.

Catering to smart brown trout cuts a rift in my person for the five months of trout season. I obsess over catching them. Any decision, even as simple as deciding when to wake up, when to turn in, or when to take my meals, I make referring to the habits of whatever old brown trout I am stalking. Their schedules determine my schedule. Their favorite foods determine the flies I tie. Water clarity and the light falling on their feeding station determine the delicacy of my tippets. All else is superfluous.

At first, I justified my hunt for large brown trout as necessary to establish my fly fishing credentials. Dedicated as I was, success came my way and word spread of my catches. My writing and my fly tying business prospered. Yet even with my reputation secure, the need to catch smart brown trout took on greater and greater urgency. Throughout my life, the hardest question for me to answer is, "Do I belong in this world of men?" I had my doubts. Consumption set me apart. I did not have the breath and strength to excel at athletics nor any career demanding great physical energy. I could not plan courses of study, become bookish, because pneumonia and its fevers interrupted my attendance, sometimes for months. And there was always the fear I might infect my fellow students. It was futile to start up or work a business that demanded regular hours. Chronic illnesses puts long-term planning on hold.

And then there is the overt discrimination against consumptives. Some railroads ban consumptives from their passenger cars. The town of Liberty, just after I arrived, made it a crime for consumptives to stay overnight within the town limits. Now that Mother and I stay winters at the Liberty House, I fear local authorities will knock on our door one night and order us out of town. And not just Liberty, other Catskill towns have passed similar ordinances. Even some churches restrict our participation as though we are lepers. Thus, every day for one reason or another, human society reminds me that I do not belong here.

Smart brown trout told me differently. Fishing for them, I wade among a lineage predating man. This most difficult quarry never succumbs to fads. They never bow to convention. They are not part of our human society but of the countryside, a more ancient world. Thus brown trout taught me to view our human society for what it was—a temporary curiosity tied to time, place, and personality, all fleeting. When I catch a smart brown trout, I come in contact with the foundations of the wild, a more permanent world. And with that understanding, I feel the pull to conduct myself in accord with the absolute and eternal, humbly accepting the meaning of my short occupation here, making my way unswayed by whim or fancy.

So each time I catch a smart brown trout, the feeling of belonging courses through me, lingering for days, warming me.

That so few other anglers catch them leads me to believe I have an extraordinary hold on this place. I, the consumptive, the shunned one, am more deeply rooted here than anyone I know. The feeling never grows stale, no matter how often I experience it.

These thoughts led me eventually to an important discovery. In the end, fishing for old brown trout is always one on one. Two individuals with their own unique histories. This realization makes my heart race. When an old brown trout spurns my fly, I retire to the bank for a deeper consideration of its unique personality. Perhaps another fly, a thinner, longer leader, a more delicate cast, a longer float, and so on. Perhaps, as a last resort, a grasshopper, stonefly, or damselfly slapped down will draw its strike. Perhaps, perhaps, perhaps.

Solving the "perhaps," I cast again and watch my fly slip down the current. As it nears the old trout's lie, the moment of truth is at hand. And my doubt returns, "Do I belong here?" The question rides the river. I wait for the take. And with the take my brown trout confirms that this countryside, its rivers, its mountains, its seasons, and its creatures embrace me as one of their own. I learn once again that I am living among my own kind.

# 18

## Jeanie's Treachery

For weeks, Jeanie pestered me to make an appointment with my doctors at the sanatorium. She gave that up when I told her the subject was "off limits." Then she pestered me to attend a Class Meeting. Each time she raised it, I met her with a pointed question about the dinner menu or some such. When I passed through the kitchen on my way to breakfast, undaunted, she sang, "In the sweet by and by, we shall meet on that beautiful shore…." I just hurried along without comment, and she finally gave up.

Lately, she takes Roy and Christian aside as they leave. I hear them through the register in my room. First was Christian. One afternoon when he was leaving for home, I heard Jeanie say, "I need a quick word with you, Christian." His "Of course" brought a muffled response. First, I heard the back door open and their steps outside. Before the door closed, I caught one word "…relatives." Their conversation on the back porch was short. Perhaps she wants another pair of pressure socks for me, I thought. Gordon Spencer sent a pair from South Orange when my legs began to swell this winter. They relieved the ache somewhat.

Jeanie reached out to Roy also. He stops most Saturdays with my mail. Last Saturday as he was leaving, I heard the same, "Roy, I need a quick word with you." Again Jeanie's voice fell to a whisper as the back door opened and closed. This time I heard nothing.

No more pressure socks came, yet the conferences continued. I heard Roy say once, "I made some calls...." And I heard Christian say once, "They weren't there...."

I believe Jeanie has broken our truce. She couldn't leave well enough alone. She has told them I am dying.

Ever since a child, I feared my next fever would kill me. The fevers came often enough, and with them, the terrors of death. Facing death so often in childhood, I grew immune to it. No need for ritual and kind thoughts. No need for Jeanie and her meetings. No need to call on courage to face the end. The moment of my death will come as anonymously as any other distracted moment of my life.

Jeanie's mistake is believing one must prepare for death. My thought is if you need to prepare for death, you wasted your life. Living as I have always lived has prepared me for my death.

# 19

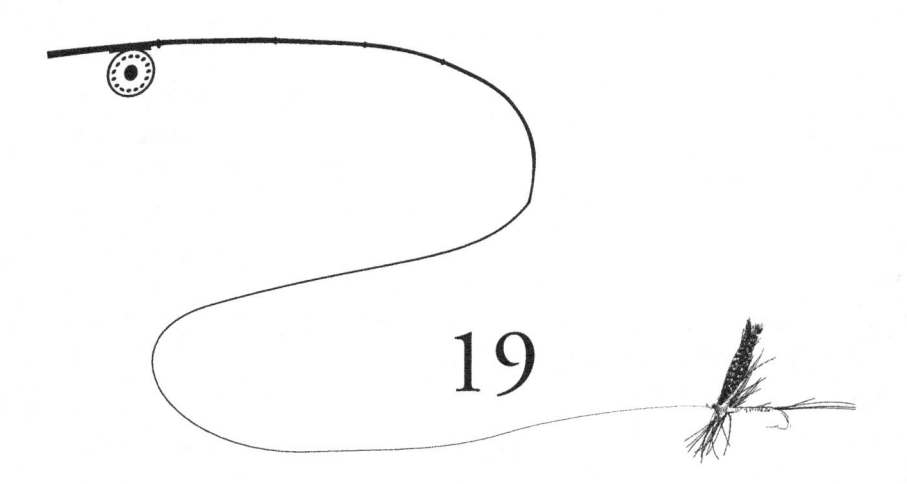

## Dinner with La Branche and Hewitt

On June 7, 1914, George Michelle La Branche and Ed Hewitt met me for dinner at the Liberty Hotel. They had just come from fishing the Roof estate on the Neversink. Private water. Their creels were full of brook trout, small fish, seven to ten inches. They were taking them back to Manhattan.

Other than fly fishing, I have little in common with La Branche and Hewitt. Both are young men, moneyed, well-traveled, and well-regarded by Manhattan society. La Branche is a stockbroker and an officer of the Anglers Club. I believe he is grooming Hewitt for club office. Hewitt is the great-grandson of Peter Cooper, inventor of the first steam locomotive and a former Mayor of New York.

The publication of Mr. La Branche's book *The Dry Fly and Fast Water* prompted the meeting. La Branche wanted a favorable review in *Forest and Stream*. Several weeks earlier, *Forest and Stream* sent me a copy of La Branche's book asking for my thoughts. Probably La Branche learned from his friends at the magazine that I would be writing the review of his book. He was anxious my review be favorable. I suspect he brought Hewitt along as a witness in case we argued. Privately, a few years earlier, we had sparred over what became the central thesis of his book. Quite by accident, we met on the Neversink. I took the opportunity to upbraid him for searching the water, especially fast water, with a dry fly when no trout were rising. I told him that it was an "affectation." Nonetheless, Hewitt's presence was unnecessary. There would be no argument, for I wrote a favorable review and had dropped it in Roy's hand at the Liberty post office on my way to dinner. All through the evening, I avoided talking about La Branche's book, keeping him guessing, toying with his curiosity so to speak. He and Hewitt hung on my every word hoping for a clue. I did not give them a hint.

Some of La Branche's theories pose problems for me. La Branche believes proper presentation is the key to fooling trout. And no wonder, the Anglers' Club is a casting club and La Branche, one of their best, wins contests for the club at its Central Park meets. He dismisses the importance of color, arguing as proof the spurious fact that trout do not perceive color. I could not endorse these positions. My experience forbids it. Additionally, over dinner, La Branche and Hewitt went one further. They took the position that for success an angler need fish but one dry fly, any dry fly, so long as it is properly presented. This position contradicted La Branche's own book and is due in part, I believe, to their success fishing private water such as the Roof estate or Hewitt's own Ringwood. Anglers' success on private waters proves nothing. For me, the most repellent of La Branche's strategies is repeatedly casting a dry fly over a known hold of a trout, thus creating what can best be described as an artificial hatch. La Branche believes if a trout sees the same pattern often enough in a short space of time, it will come to believe it natural food and strike. To my mind, this is a form of chumming, "scientific" chumming, but chumming nonetheless.

With the help of a several dozen oysters on the half shell and a few glasses of brandy, the conversation flowed freely from the start. They were enthusiastic about Roof's water. Testing their newest theory, they confined themselves to one dry fly pattern each. For La Branche, his Pink Lady, and for Hewitt, a Tup's Indispensable. They'd caught over a hundred fish in two days and so believed their theory proven. For my part, rather than disagree, I questioned them, playing the part of a wide-eyed greenhorn. They described the water on the Roof's estate at length. It sounded similar to the water I fished near Claryville. I knew well the Pink Lady and the Tup's patterns. I sell Pink Ladies to La Branche. As for the Tup's, I related to them how Skues sent me the fly and a sample of its secret dubbing. I apologized for not giving them the dubbing formula claiming Skues swore me to secrecy. I did not tell them I never had much luck with either fly. The discussion turned to casting. I am not as proficient as La Branche. It does not matter. These days Christian casts for me, and I believe him as good a caster as La Branche. This also was left unsaid.

"Have you ever fished the Roof estate?" Hewitt asked.

Laughing, I launched into one of my oft-repeated stories. "Yes... quite by accident. Although the property's posted, I was too intent on fishing to notice the signs when I waded into Roof's water. One of Roof's gamekeepers discovered me, and after accusing me of trespassing, escorted me off the estate, verbally abusing me all the while." I mimicked the frenzy of the gamekeeper. Neither smiled.

La Branche said, "Ownership has its privileges."

Hewitt offered to intervene with Roof. "We'll get you an invitation."

"No need. I'll be spending next month on the Beaverkill." More a hope than a firm plan. A day of wading the Beaverkill knocked me out, labored breathing, heart racing, sometimes chest pains. Frequent rest stops helped, but it took so long for me to recover that most of my day was spent sitting on boulders and observing the water.

Halford had died two months earlier. Looking about the table, I reminded them of his death, adding, "We three owe him so much."

They agreed, but it was Hewitt, the engineer, who ticked off Halford's many scientific contributions to fly fishing, ending with, "We should support more efforts applying science to fly fishing. I can think of so many subjects needing inquiry. The physiology of the trout, the biology of its habitat, stream enhancement, pisciculture, further studies of entomology, and not just of the sub imago and the imago stages of aquatic insects in American rivers and lakes, but of the earlier stages of development. Skues has written a book about fishing nymphs. We should follow up on his discoveries."

"Ed, you're not suggesting that we should fish wet flies. Skues is an aberrant. We cannot follow him down that path."

"Of course not, George, but we should keep an open mind on how science can improve fly fishing. Don't you agree Mr. Gordon?"

"I am not trained in science, so I will leave that to better heads than mine. Yours, for instance."

"What do you think of the Neversink, Mr. Gordon? Do you like it?"

I began tentatively. "Yes. It has the same caddis and mayflies the Beaverkill has. Some Junes we even get a Green Drake emergence. It's spotty but memorable. Other insect hatches are prolific. Sure, there is the cycle of flood and drought as with other Catskill rivers, but we're higher up here, and the river stays cooler longer. What can I say? The Neversink suits me."

"Do you correspond with Skues?" La Branche asked.

This was dangerous water. "Yes, just as I corresponded with Halford during his life."

"You corresponded with Halford?"

"Yes. Once he sent me four dozen of his own flies. They're tied according to the dressings given in his first book."

"Did you read his last work?" Hewitt interjected.

"Yes."

"What did you think of it?"

"Quite honestly, there was nothing new in it. Not that a book need be novel to be worthwhile. His *Entomology* alone justifies his place in the history of fly fishing."

"So, you're critical of Halford?"

"No. Of course not. As I say, we owe him much. I reread all

his books almost every year, and sometimes after a luckless day fishing, I flip through one or the other of them for an idea."

"How would you compare Halford's books with mine, Mr. Gordon?" La Branche asked.

A smile played across my lips. "His are longer."

Hewitt laughed. La Branche, ever serious, sat quietly. I winked at him and said, "More to the point, you build on Halford...as does Skues. I do not believe there is anyone living who could contribute anything as comprehensive as what Halford left us. His genius touched everything. Can any of us honestly claim to be his equal?"

"When you put it that way, of course not."

"Is there any other way to put it?"

La Branche grimaced but managed, "No."

"Don't you believe more comprehensive treatises will come with further scientific breakthroughs?" Hewitt asked.

I nodded and La Branche said enthusiastically, "You're just the man for it, Ed."

By then, I had worked through my prime rib. La Branche signaled the waiter. "What are you serving in the way of desserts?"

"We have a dessert cart." The waiter left to wheel it over.

I chose the chocolate layer cake with butter cream frosting. Before the waiter left, La Branche asked, "Would you be so good as to bring us a few more brandies?"

"Of course, sir."

More brandy...to loosen my tongue? La Branche does not know that the more I drink the more guarded I become. At the Brooklyn Fly Fisher's clubhouse, whiskey fuels all sorts of good-natured arguments, lies, and earnest political discussion. As for political discussions, I fall silent, attentive but remote. If pressed, I say I am too young to remember the Civil War, a time when many of the founders of the club became Republicans. After the war, some ran for office in Brooklyn on the Republican ticket. I was raised a Jeffersonian Democrat, a dwindling minority in the North, and nothing I care to confess to club members. I sell them flies and contribute to fishing discussions. When late night discussions turn to politics, however, I plead fatigue and find a quiet bed in the dormitory. About the only Northerner with whom I feel comfortable discussing politics is Charles Orvis, another Jeffersonian Democrat. Traveling the South, it was to my credit that my political views coincided with the views of so many of my relatives and acquaintances. No, large amounts of alcohol will not loosen my tongue. If the Brooklyn Fly Fishers whiskey could not, La Branche and his snifters of brandy certainly will not.

"Where do you think fly fishing is going, Mr. Gordon?" La Branche asked.

"I hate guessing. Living in the country for the last ten years, I rarely visit the city, so I am unacquainted with the scientific fly fishers you meet daily."

Turning to Hewitt for reassurance, La Branche said, "We understand it's just speculation. Let me start by saying I believe fly fishing's becoming cruder."

"I'm unaware of that trend," I began. La Branche looked at me sharply. Time to back-pedal. "Yes, well, to get to your question, I believe two things are happening. As more people move west, fly fishers discover more and more trout water, waters too numerous for any one angler to explore in a lifetime. Having fished most of the Catskill rivers and many streams in Pennsylvania, Vermont, New Hampshire, and Maine, I now fish only two, the Neversink and the Beaverkill. I feel at home on them. For me, the game comes down to fooling difficult trout. Nothing is more satisfying than catching a smart, large brown trout on a fly of my own devising. So I spend my time haunting the Neversink and Beaverkill looking for large brown trout. That is my game. It is not everyone's game. Others will find other types of water more congenial. As I see it, the fly fishing experience is becoming more diverse. This is not surprising. American waters are so very diverse."

"I would rather fish the British chalk streams," La Branche said wistfully. "I believe that water would suit me."

Hewitt jumped in, "When I was younger and inexperienced, I fished a few British chalk streams. Going back with what I know now could be instructive. Something to write about. Maybe in time I will become wedded to certain waters. Who knows? Maybe I'll camp out on the Neversink like you, Mr. Gordon."

"You said you saw two things happening," La Branche said.

"Yes. More and more local people are taking up fly fishing. Two of the best fly fishers I know are farmers. Previously, it was only wealthy people like Halford, people like yourselves, who could afford fly fishing. Ordinary people could not afford the cost of equipment, travel, club fees, and the time. But all that is changing. There is a new mood in the country. America promises all its people access to the arts, education, and so forth. It is one of the reasons our country is so great. These rivers about here will become more and more crowded with fly fishers. I see it steadily building. Some of the locals are very skilled, and they will become more and more skilled as the fish become more and more wary. In time the most skilled anglers will be local fly fishers, tradesmen, farmers, mechanics, clerks, and so forth. It is they who will set the tone of our sport."

"But they have no understanding of our traditions and literature," La Branche forcefully interjected.

"You'd be surprised. Fly fishing forces its enthusiasts to read. The successful locals read Halford, Skues, and the fly fishing articles in *Forest and Stream*, for instance. New fishing and hunting magazines start up every day, some deal with fly fishing for trout." Smiling broadly, I turned to La Branche and said, "They will even read your book."

"But will they read it in the right spirit?" La Branche made a face. "I doubt it."

"I have great hopes for our local fly fishers...men and women."

La Branche was not won over. So I asked, "I sent you a gray fly which I designed with you in mind. Have you had any luck with it?"

"Actually, you sent me a dozen of the pattern, and I offered several to friends to test. It has been a success. I still use the Whirling Blue Dun but have had some extraordinary days fishing your fly. Of course, its success is due in great part to my casting skills. My friends now call your fly the La Branche."

Carefully, I replied, "Of course....I'm honored to be associated with your name." La Branche smiled and sat back

A thoroughly enjoyable meal. And they paid the bill. As we parted on the front porch, Hewitt asked plainly, "Well, what do you think of La Branche's book?" I smiled, thanked them for the evening, and told them, "You can read my review in the next issue of *Forest and Stream*."

"Can't you give us a hint?"

"You have been very kind so I will tell you that it is a good thing Mr. La Branche is an American." This enigmatic answer puzzled them. I struck off down Liberty Street, leaving them on the hotel porch with frowns on their faces. Yes, the evening was delightful.

I wrote a positive review of *Fast Water*, even though the differences between La Branche and me are considerable. His certitude about all things trout galls me. He follows Halford's precepts unquestioningly. Thus, his book lacks originality. What led me to look favorably on La Branche's book was its appearance coincident with Halford's death. With Halford silent, I saw the rise of a fully independent school of American fly fishing. In my review, I listed the American authors who had preceded La Branche to demonstrate that his book came out of a fifty-year tradition of American writing on fly fishing. I might disagree with La Branche's positions on many issues, but we shared what I will call the American attitude, a versatile approach to fly fishing. For that reason, and that reason alone, I supported his book.

It was not the first time I took such a forgiving view of an

American fishing author. Two years previous, Emlyn Gill's book *Practical Dry Fly Fishing* was published. Gill's views also conflicted with my own. He believed that British entomology and British fly patterns were sufficient for American anglers; that no American writer had previously explained dry fly fishing; and that Frederick Halford was the last word on fly fishing. He was wrong on all three points. I could have taken Gill to task publicly. But did not. I had a front row seat to the vicious fight between Halford and Skues. Their debate pitted British anglers against each other and even led to Skue's expulsion from his fishing club. I made the decision not to import such conflicts to America. Displays of animosity among writers will raise magazine circulation and put the names of the combatants before the public. But I will have no part of it. Discourse among anglers should be civil in the tradition of Uncle Thad and Father Izaak.

# 20

## Plans for Writing a Book

As my health deteriorates, I spend more time in bed. Sometimes for days. My final years are at hand. In a year or two, I will be an invalid without the strength to tie flies for the market. Time on the river experimenting with new flies will be out of the question. Writing is my only hope for income. I find it less taxing. Many ideas pop into my head, and if I could write them all down, my future would be assured. I do not want to fall back on my relatives. They would have me return to West Haverstraw where they could more easily care for me. But I would miss these mountains and their rivers. From my window, I watch the Neversink flow past, season after season. Seeing the light play over it during the course of a day soothes me.

My writing has gone through many changes. These last years, it exhibits a calm. When reading the ignorance spread by so many, I remind myself that I have spent more time fly fishing than any of them. For certain, I have spent more time fly fishing for trout than any of our scientific anglers, La Branche, Gill, and Rhead. My wealth of experience is my touchstone. Raising my voice issuing angry dismissive essays is futile. It simply generates other loud voices and more angry words. The cure for ignorance and so the cure for dogma is fishing public waters for difficult trout. There, success is hard won. There, the winning strategy can never be reduced to a pet theory.

So I argue for more experience. That is my only real cause. Instead of debating about fishing, I urge my readers to fish. Inexperienced anglers spout theories. Experienced anglers recount details. I believe that once La Branche gains more experience, hopefully on public waters, he will discard his single dry fly, repetitive presentation theory. Some critics have held it against me that I never wrote a book. The fact is I have published more than any of the scientific anglers including La Branche. Taken together my publications total more pages than any of my contemporaries other than Halford.

Instead of writing more magazine pieces, a new kind of writing takes shape in my mind. Like most anglers I enjoy fishing stories more than works of fishing instruction. A serialized story in *Forest and Stream* gave me a clue to the sort of book I should write. The story is entitled, "Where the Barefoot Boys Look for Trout." Winfield T. Sherwood is its author, and it was serialized over seven issues beginning in January of 1909. The first installment reenacted a tavern scene, a May evening, on the Esopus River. Both young and old, experienced and inexperienced anglers figure as characters. It was an evening of whiskey drinking and storytelling before a roaring fire, reminiscent of my evenings with the Brooklyn Fly Fishers. One character, a middle aged urban professional taught himself to cast but had no luck fishing. His problem was he did not know where the fish were. In Sherwood's tale, the Barefoot Boys, men who grew up in the country, fished with worms as boys. Worm fishing taught them where trout hold. and so as fly fishers they could coach the neophyte where to locate trout on the Esopus. They recommended the use of both dry and wet flies depending on the water. Swift water, riffles and rapids, calls for wet flies; pools and runs can be fished profitably with dry flies.

In his story Sherwood mentions me. So I recommend the article to all, a bit of vanity on my part. At first, Sherwood considered placing his story on the Beaverkill but did not do so because I, the acknowledged expert on the Beaverkill according to him, had written so beautifully about the river. Thus Sherwood moved the action to the Esopus out of deference.

An entertaining fishing book would sell. As I conceive it, the book would incorporate a string of anecdotes unified by a few common themes of instruction. Skues' latest works have freed me from the comprehensive format Halford pioneered. When I think of writing a book I think of Skues' book, *Minor Tactics of the Chalk Stream* in which he wrote of specific solutions to specific problems attending dry fly fishing. His tactics generally involved wet flies cast upstream. My book would follow a similar structure with one difference. I will expand on the anecdotes, developing the personalities of the anglers, their conversations, their frustrations, and the character of the river. My book will both entertain and instruct. The entertainment will compel the readers' interest, and the instruction will win their gratitude.

To all my angler friends I recommend without reservation W. C. Prime's *I Go A-Fishing*. A popular New York author, Prime includes in his fishing tales many personal reminiscences. He tells of lovers won and lost, faith, friendship, travel, fishing, triumphs and failures. He fished most of Europe, the Holy Land, and of course New York and New England. His books prove the point that the best fishing books are not just about fishing. Prime takes Walton's contemplative angler to the extreme. The reader travels the globe before finishing up a day fishing with Prime.

Another author I admire is Henry Van Dyke. Like Prime Van Dyke's fishing stories run the full range of topics: faith, the beauty of women, world history, the habits of trout, geology, and literature. Van Dyke fished New Jersey, the Adirondacks, and the Catskills as well as the most famous European trout waters. A professor of religion and literature at Princeton University, Van Dyke enriched such essays as his "Little Rivers" with literary allusions, personal reminiscences, and original poetry. I agree with Van Dyke and Prime that the seemingly extraneous reflections an angler entertains while out fishing are what fishing is about.

My books will differ from Sherwood's on the one hand and Prime's and Van Dyke's on the other. I will include more dramatic detail than Sherwood whose story becomes more and more weighted down with fly fishing instruction as it moved along. On the other hand my books will include more instruction than Prime and Van Dyke provide in theirs. Often their fishing excursions bog down in tangential stories of famous places and people. They assume their audience knows the intricacies of fly fishing. I will not make that mistake. My book will artfully blend the novelistic with fly fishing techniques so neither predominate. It will sell. I am sure of it. And I will not need to leave my bed.

## 21

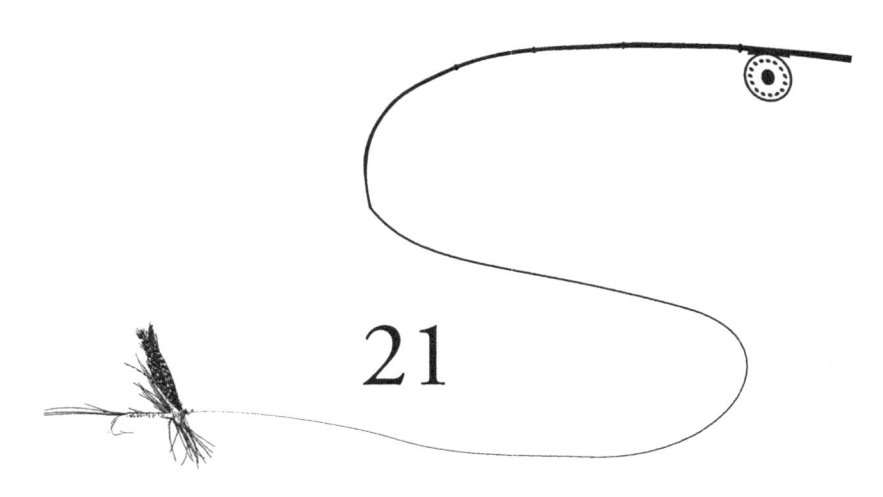

## Dinner with Mrs. Henderson

For most of my life, consumption hunted me. It never confronts its victims openly until the very end. Rather it lures them to waste their health. Consumption dives into their deepest yearnings, into that limitless well of hope its victims call their future. It is in looking ahead that consumption joins them as a treacherous ally. They search for a new land, one with magical air which, with each intake of breath, swells their lungs to health. Thoreau followed consumption's call to Minnesota. Exhausted, his passion to travel spent, he grew fearful and hurried back to Concord without staying for the cure. Weakened and vulnerable, he died within the year.

I understand Thoreau's fear. I dread the day when smothered by starched white sheets and heavy comforters I lack the strength to throw back my covers. All about me a subterranean dark, I, no more than a pebble subducted by catastrophic forces, soon to be amalgamated, sealed up forever in a lifeless chamber. Sapped of strength, wedged tight, I panic to claw my way out. Breadth expelled and so compacted, I lay hemmed in on all sides, clinging to the fleeting hope that millennia from now anonymous forces will extrude me as some schist, swaddled in inertia. No longer the piece worker making his quota.

This winter's bouts of swelling ankles and hoarse coughing grow more frequent and slow my tying. So many flies tied per hour, per day, per month. Every morning the laundress picks up her iron knowing the number of sheets, shirts, dresses she must press to feed her family. Every morning I fix a hook in my vise knowing the number of flies I must tie to continue boarding here by the Neversink. The day is not far off when I will no longer be able to make that number. More coughing. A sip of water, a swipe of a newly bleached rag across my stained lips. Gradually coming back to myself, I calculate the number of flies left to tie. I never lose track of the number, for the number is what must be. So I spend longer days and nights at my vice, starkly aware that if I do not make my number, I will lose my grip on this world. A penniless old man, I fear. Anonymous, I fear.

As I struggle here, so Mother struggles in South Orange. Consumption infected her long before my entrance into this world. She spent her early years cataloging its career. Colds and bronchitis, with pneumonia not far off. Fever, prolonged coughing and labored breathing, then bed rest and, if it should come, recovery after weeks of convalescence. When, as a child, I showed the first signs of respiratory distress, my mother withdrew me from school and was criticized for being too protective. She ignored the criticisms and no doubt saved my life. I will always be grateful.

For all our exertions, Mother and I lose ground every year. Our breathing becomes shallower, and our energy for the simplest tasks wanes. Constantly reminded of our frailty, we fall victim to consumption's temptations. We feel the frantic urge to travel, and forgetting the history of our struggles, we preoccupy ourselves with setting destinations, packing, and travel. It is all a distraction. And together we experience the disappointing aftermath, the malaise, when our diseased ambitions drain us of all strength. No need to admit our foolishness. In its secret language consumption taunts us and crushed, we, its captives, hear deep within its victory song celebrating our defeat. All that is left, a weary glance, a resigned waive from sick bed signaling surrender.

As a child, my mother encouraged me with the example of my father's strength. Growing up, I knew him only as the face looking out from a dozen photographs, the mythic hero of my mother's stories. Yearning to know him, I spent time studying his portraits, daguerreotypes encased in ornate silver frames. His steady, confident eyes encouraged me. They said, "Stand fast." So unlike the person I see staring out from my photographs. That person pleads, "What do you see? Please tell me, I would like to know." Suspicion is there; fear is there. Too many defeats have made me wary.

Years ago, Mother and I visited Magnetic Springs in Michigan. Its claims for the healing properties of its waters were extravagant, and our own consumption vouched for them. Excited, we took musty trains to where an open carriage jolted rutted, sandy roads through a lush rural countryside to the spa, a new large frame building, white and rambling. Its tiled spring house was damp and smelled of sulphur. Pew like mahogany benches flanked by marble topped tables circled a bubbling fountain and brass grated drains. From silver trays uniformed attendants served mineral water, and three times a day Mother and I drank it. By the third day, I grew bored. Mother followed the spa's regimen faithfully. She believed in the cure. She always believed in the cure.

A large pond, more a reservoir, bordered the spa. Walking to and from the spring house, I saw fish splashing by its dam. The manager of the spa gave me permission to take out one of their rowboats. "Bring back your catch. We'll cook them up for you." The pond, long and narrow, followed the course of an old stream bed. Drowned trees died gaunt in its waters. Wending my way through them, I rowed the length of the pond to where its stream entered. There I caught a few small native trout, too small to keep. Shipping my oars, I drifted slowly back downstream casting a large Bumblepuppy alongside the dead trees. Counting ten before retrieving in short, swift jerks, I caught black bass after black bass.

By the time the manager helped me slide the rowboat ashore, its bottom was ankle deep in fish. "You've enough for yourself and our guests. It will be a nice change. Do you mind if we offer them on the menu tonight."

"Not at all."

"I will reduce your bill accordingly. And tomorrow if you catch more I will reduce it even further."

The remainder of our stay was *gratis*. Just as well because the waters did not work a cure. Another of consumption's cruel jokes.

Last day of trout season, evening, a few trout fed in Henderson's pool. The water was low, and small brown caddis flies were emerging. Trout slashed for them. I caught several pound and a half brown trout on a Mink fly. Sensing a presence behind me, I turned. Mrs. Henderson was watching from the bank.

"Whenever you're nearby Mr. Gordon, my taste for trout sharpens."

Looking up at her shapely figure, I nodded. I was not looking forward to the walk back to Liberty in the dark. Dinner and a bed at the Henderson's were preferable even if I was condemned to spend the evening alone with Mrs. Henderson.

"Happy to oblige, Mrs. Henderson. What I have in my creel will make a banquet."

"It's only cook and me."

"Sam?"

'Sam's in the city meeting a shipment of hides from Argentina."

"Ann?"

"Ann's given notice. She is betrothed to the son of a shop owner in Livingston Manor and needs time to assemble her trousseau."

"She was...a...very efficient," Choosing a virtue I believed Mrs. Henderson would appreciate.

"She was more than efficient," Mrs. Henderson said curtly. She lowered her head and said "I will miss her." Her voice betrayed more emotion than I expected.

Unprepared for this turn, I waded ashore and held my creel up to her without comment.

Mrs. Henderson waived it aside, "Mr. Gordon if you would be so kind, take my trout to our cook, Karen, by yourself."

Slippers in hand, Karen collected me from the summer kitchen and led me to the dining room where Mrs. Henderson sat at the dinner table absent-mindedly twirling the stem of a glass of sherry.

A sherry stood in the place opposite her. I took my seat and after a sip said, "I wish to say I'm very sorry to hear about Ann leaving."

"Don't be. I've taken on her family. Good people, educated people, who immigrated here from Kilmallock near Limerick, Ireland where Ann's father taught school. Once here, the father contracted and, in short order, succumbed to consumption." Looking directly at me, she said matter-of-factly, "You're intimately familiar with the disease, I believe, Mr. Gordon."

"If I had stayed working on Wall Street, I would not be enjoying your sherry this evening."

"Yes. Yes. Ann is gone, but I hired her sister to take her place. She's due in Liberty tomorrow to help me close up for the season. Sam hired one of her brothers. The young man aspires to be an accountant. Both are bright."

"It was good of you."

"Nonsense. We will profit from their employment."

I did not entirely accept Mrs. Henderson's resort to business as the motive for her kindness. Plainly she valued Ann for more than her work. "She was a willing worker," I offered to further draw her out.

"More importantly she did not carry tales. I could speak freely in front of her. So many tradesman, household help, even friends and relatives pass on slander. Ann was loyal. A rare quality."

Cook brought a basket of fresh dinner rolls and two platters, one with the poached trout, the other with buttered mashed potatoes and glazed carrots. She placed them down between Mrs. Henderson and me. "Anything else, Ma'am?"

"No Karen. This will do."

Mrs. Henderson gestured toward me, "Help yourself Mr. Gordon. Pretend you are at one of your boarding houses."

I caught a sarcastic edge to her voice, so I inquired, "Would you allow me to serve you?"

Taken aback, she said, "Why thank you, Mr. Gordon."

Standing at her left shoulder, I asked, "A whole trout, Mrs. Henderson?"

"Yes. Against my will you're making me reassess you, Mr. Gordon."

"That's not my intention," I said forking a trout onto her plate. "You have my measure, I believe." After spooning out a portion of potatoes and carrots for her, I sat down, "Have you any questions for me?"

She smiled. "Sam left none. But if you'll indulge me, I have one of my own. It is of a personal nature, and I bring it up simply out of curiosity. I would not be offended if you refused to answer. Everyone is entitled to their privacy."

"What is your question?"

"Last time you stayed with us, you recited a stanza of poetry from Sidney Lanier to describe the many doubts which afflict you when you're writing. When pressed, you gave the impression you mourned a lost love."

"Yes," I said cautiously.

"Am I to understand that you failed to win her over?"

"No. Just the opposite," I hesitated, "I drove her away." Searching for the right words to explain, my silence lengthened.

"You needn't say more if it is too painful, Mr. Gordon."

"It is painful. But that is not what stops me. I am searching for how to tell you." As in surrender I waved a fork with a carrot on it. Catching myself, I glanced at Mrs. Henderson, smiled, glanced again at the carrot and laughed. Mrs. Henderson smiled and laughed with me. I put my fork down. "It's a story I'm sure you've heard before. Gail, that was her name, and I were very much in love but arrived at an impasse planning our future. She wanted to venture west. I wanted to stay here. The dilemma paralyzed me. As it was, time passing made the choice for us. I stayed here, and she moved on. What I wrestle with now are the deeper reasons for my reluctance to go with her."

"What was her western venture?"

"Her father owned a profitable lumber company, and he offered the two of us positions running its headquarters in Michigan. On our combined salaries we could have a family, save money, buy property, and grow wealthy. Very likely Gail would have inherited the business when her father passed."

"To me the right choice seems obvious. What stopped you from going west with her?"

"That is what I struggle to understand. At first I believed I was a coward, afraid of living in a place without starched napkins." Helplessly I looked over at Mrs. Henderson. "But I was given only a half a day to make up my mind, and I rebelled at being stampeded into a decision." I paused searching my thoughts again, "What I think now is that I feared losing my independence. This, I believe, is closer to the truth."

"Wealth brings independence," said Mrs. Henderson, clearly dismayed. My mind was back in the dusty road fronting Herron's so I did not respond immediately. Impatient she prompted me, "Don't you agree Mr. Gordon?"

"It is my observation that wealth comes with its own demands. The greater the wealth, the greater the demands. Meeting those demands leaves one little independence."

Mrs. Henderson was quick to respond, "Contending with the obligations of the rich I find far less threatening than worrying about life's essentials."

"For me the choice was not between being rich or poor. The choice was between keeping my innermost thoughts to myself or handing them over to Gail whenever she asked. No secret vices mind you, just keeping my own counsel, free of criticism from any quarter. In the end I decided not to give up the absolute freedom of my innermost self. Married, Gail would have had the right to expect that I would be forthright with her. It has always been my nature to hold back as you have pointed out more than once. Any efforts by her to trespass on my inner secrets would fester and in time poison our marriage."

"You could have become more open."

"No, Mrs. Henderson. I see no value in revealing my deepest thoughts and feelings on demand. Most are not fully formed, and I abhor speaking half-truths."

"The alternative, reduced circumstances, I believe is worse," Mrs. Henderson offered patiently.

"Loneliness is my punishment for not going with Gail. I've no wife, no family, no children, but I am not the only angler so afflicted. Such is the condition of my friend Mr. Skues, the London barrister. I deal with the pain of loneliness, as he does, by staying fully engaged. Loneliness comes in force once the sun goes down. So now at night I tie flies, write letters and call to mind better times until, exhausted, I fall asleep."

Mrs. Henderson added kindly, "It is fortunate that you have fishing to console you."

Her sensitivity touched me. "Mrs. Henderson, I do not wish to seem contentious tonight, but fishing provides no solace for life's problems. It cannot repair a broken rod tip; it cannot mend a broken heart; it cannot fill an empty bank account."

"Mr. Gordon, I believe you are wrong. Fishing provides diversion from life's day to day problems. Fishing gives the overworked respite. I know I don't sound like the same person who took you to task for luring men back to their boyhood, but I see the effect of fly fishing on Sam. He takes a few hours off to fish and comes back with renewed energy and a new perspective."

"I'm happy to hear it's working out for you and Sam. Let me say, however, I agree with the position you took that night a while ago when you dissected my articles. The truth is, as you then argued, fishing is useless except for an occasional entree, a meal which can be more cheaply purchased from the local grocer.

Leaning back Mrs. Henderson wagged her head, "Mr. Gordon you surprise me."

Contritely, I said, "I'm sorry to say the argument you make tonight in favor of fly fishing has never satisfied me. The strongest arguments for fly fishing rest on the supposition that fly fishing is a world unto itself, an impractical world which cannot be fully managed to our ends. It is my firm belief that fly fishing owes us nothing."

A smile played over her lips, "So Mr. Gordon, one of my discarded arguments against fishing has now won you over.""

"You can be very persuasive when I already agree with you."Mrs. Henderson laughed, as I continued,. "Fly fishing is a world complete within itself...a fully self-contained, self-confirming good. By grasping a fly rod and waiving it like a wizard's wand, fly fishers conjure up this autonomous world, a world of the ever fresh...the ever new...the ever surprising. In a word, the swish... swish of rod, line, and fly conjures up wonder, that indispensable and, I would argue, that rarest commodity our world has to offer. In wonder the dedicated fly fisher embraces the new with a patient mind, a mind willing to entertain ambiguity for years until that time when, if ever, absolute clarity dawns. Spend a day fly fishing and you'll be confused and surprised. Spend a lifetime fly fishing and you'll lead a life of doubt and wonder."

"That may be Mr. Gordon, but why can't you also admit fly fishing is a healthy diversion?"

"Because it's not true. Calling fly fishing a diversion makes it nothing more than a way to pass time, a pointless enterprise, a waste, unworthy of one's best efforts and talents. Striving, as I do to excel,

I admit no exceptions to living by the highest standards. And that is why fly fishing suits me. Fly fishing demands its adherents work at being worthy of it. It demands fly fishers develop the highest skills and greatest understanding, and only when they do, will it reward them by drawing them deeper and deeper into wonder. "

I looked over to Mrs. Henderson for a response. "You have not convinced me yet," she said. "I am waiting."

I smiled. "Wonder is my purpose. It's what sustains me. It's what draws my eyes to the river every morning. On occasion I, as other dedicated fly fishers, live whole days in wonder. No longer aware of the passing hours, our unencumbered minds become stranded in the moment. That place of far horizons. That place where the what of us that went before, the what of us that lives in the here and now, and the what of us that looks ahead, meet and converse. So we keep casting, and in the swish…swish, the to and fro of rod, line, and fly, our minds reach back, hesitate, and then power forward memories dropping them curling into our timeless present where the fly comes to rest on the breast of a river pregnant with the hardly likely. So many memories, so many expectations, leisurely considered in wonder while out fly fishing."

I was about to continue when I looked over at Mrs. Henderson who appeared quizzical. "Don't mind me," she said. "What you say triggers old memories."

"Let me add one last thought." I said. "As you may surmise, I will never understand anglers who promise to make fly fishing totally predictable. Without wonder, fly fishing becomes just one more joyless engineering project."

Mrs. Henderson sat silent, staring ahead through the front windows at the darkly flowing Neversink. She said almost in a whisper, "I am thinking of Lady Campbell and similar conversations we had when I was a young girl. I did not understand her at the time." Then turning back to me she said, "May I call you Theodore?"

"Of course."

"Theodore, you may call me Adeline." She stood up and covering her mouth stifled a yawn. With a smile, she said, "Theodore, I am tired and have much on which to meditate. If you will see yourself to the kitchen, Karen will make you milk punch and show you to Ann's old room. I'll take my leave now," she said bowing.

I stood up and bowed in return. "You pamper me, Adeline." Mrs. Henderson smiled again but this time enigmatically, more to herself than to me, and was gone.

So with this memory and the press of my quota, I again tie flies in Jeanie's kitchen. The last mailer sealed and the stove damped down, my vise, hooks, letters, feathers and threads go into a cardboard box. Breathing heavily, I bend down and roll up the red splotched news pages scattered about and add them to the fire, all turning to black ash. Perhaps this Opening Day will restore my strength. And the glinting waters of the Neversink will dispel my fears.

## 22

## Coma

My memories but my waking hours laundered in shadow, stored in dream. The work of an aged mind dimming, losing its grip. Faithfully the dark sits vigil, night after night scrubbing the life out of my days. I hear its sibilant breathing. And dropping off to sleep, I feel its dry kiss as it joins me to walk the scenes of my life, my tableaux, replayed night after night on my midway of dreams.

One after another, the tableaux light up, barkers yelling, "On your left, the legendary trout. On your right, Jeanie's roast grouse. Hurry, hurry, hurry, just ahead Habersham serving Madeira in his study, June days on the Beaverkill, and the bright colors of Savannah's City Market."

Tonight I am looking for one. It is the tableau of Gail and me lying in the bark peeler's stable. Jealous, the dark jostles me roughly towards a Savannah memory, Factor's Walk and the smell of wet cotton bales and tarred rope after a warm August rain. I shrug it off and dismiss its almost realities, for I am listening for one spiel above the others. And there it is, "Step right up. Step right up. Behind this curtain you'll see the love birds. Only a dime. A thin dime. You'll see love and heroism, secrecy and cowardice. It is all here, Ladies and Gentlemen. You'll see disappointment but you will not be disappointed. A tale of doomed love." I pull the curtain aside and stand transfixed for hours until the barker touches my elbow and shoos me away. "You've gotten your dimes worth, Buddy." One last look as I turn to go, and seeing Gail's upraised arm flecked with gold, I groan.

More barkers hawk my decline, "Money worries; you've never seen such money worries. Step right up, step right up. See cold and hunger. See eviction. See blood on the snow. Hurry now or you'll miss the frozen heap of rags lying in the road." All my fears were there. The old and the new. Sick beds, ice baths, days wasted with fever, months traveling for a cure. So much wasted time searching for a deep breath. So many hours too weak to talk, to tie flies, to read, to fish. More of late. Bank statements showing little activity and few healthy balances. Harsh voices in the gloom reminding me of the desolation behind and the desolation to come.

Before my aged mind can mobilize, a punishing wind flattens and scatters my midway. "Your days are running out," the dark screams. "Clinging to Gail won't postpone the final reckoning." It lays a cold hand on my forehead and says, "There, there old man, Gail cannot save you."

Untangling tents and poles, driving stakes back into the turf, and lashing the guy lines, I raise my midway again. Angrily, I shout, "Night after night you swallow up my day in shadow. Now you attack my dreams. Will you leave me nothing?"

"Your days are phantasms. Face up to it. I'm saving you from living a lie, something you've worked your whole life to perfect, something that now must end."

"You have a weakness. I see that now. My wakeful present threatens you."

"No, old man, you have it backwards. It is you who live under threat. Your eyes dim, your hearing grows faint. You pretend to hold on knowing all the while your life is slipping away. I'm your future. You know that. Soon you will have no memory to record your waking hours. Then you'll learn that your lucid moments, your flies, your fish, your passion for Gail, all, all are illusions. I'll be all that's left. This is a hard truth. Yet a truth you know, a truth you must embrace if you wish to find peace."

"No. There is more."

Its cold breath and merciless presence pants, "You'll soon rethink your words. In the end oblivion is all there is."

"No," I sigh.

"You're provoking me."

"You've pushed me too far. Years of your dark thoughts have robbed me of bright spring mornings where each tree, each flower, each pool, each iridescent fish, and each accurate cast stands out fresh and sharply distinct. You've robbed me of the fertile smell of May meadows, of the warmth of Gail's passion. You've robbed me of being startled by the song of the White Throated Sparrow, of grazing cows ripping up new grass, of the soothing lilt of sparkling riffles. Asleep, I want to dream of plucking a stalk of new grass and for once tasting, really tasting, its yellow meat. I want to go to sleep and feel, really feel, a creel on my shoulder and hear, really hear, the snap of a fly box lid as it closes. I want to call up dusk on the Beaverkill, fluttering mayflies back lit glowing pink and see, really see, leisurely rising trout."

"I am your true friend, the only truth you'll ever know. All you value now will end in oblivion. The sooner you realize that the better."

"What I choose to know now is my unfolding present, not from moment to moment, but in a single vision. All the joys, all the disappointments, my days afield, my days with Gail, all the good and all the bad in a single sublime moment. You fear this, for it will destroy your hold on me." I heard a catch in its breathing. "For now I make do with my dreams. Sometimes pleasurable, sometimes grotesque, sometimes frightening. Always perfect, the bleached geometry of my days, the perfection of line and arc, the linear perfection of a straight red pine tree climbing a hundred feet into the heavens, the curved perfection of a fish's leap, the undulating perfection of low mountains rising and falling on a far horizon, like bird song, like Gail lying out, hips, waist, breasts and shoulders, rising and falling, a lifetime of discovery. I revel in her perfection."

A laugh. "You foolish old man. You're beginning to believe your own lies. It's pathetic the way you hang onto illusion, a child wanting one more story before closing its eyes."

"Gail was interested in me, said I was a gentleman. She believed in my talent and wanted to share her life with me." I gasped for breath.

"You may not believe this, Theodore. But I too am interested in you. If you could just discard the make believe, you would grow to love me more than you ever loved Gail."

"She believed in my future. You don't."

"Let me relieve you of that burden. It makes no difference if you have a future or not. What difference will it make, living on a few more years in Bradley or Liberty or some other Catskill village? Wouldn't it be better to be gone from these mountains? Gone from the minds of Christian and Roy, the minds of Jeanie and Anson, the minds of your correspondents."

An ominous pause, "Indulge me. Imagine yourself gone. Explore what difference your absence would make? There will be a church service, a few kind words, a very few, and then you will be forgotten. Bruce will pick up your noble rooster. Your things will be boxed and shipped, and your room let. That's your "real future." What difference if it happens now or later? No children to remember you, your flies eaten by moths, your magazine articles filed away in archives never to be read again. I see your relatives divvying up your rods and reels and burning all your papers, all your bird skins, all your animal pelts on the remote chance consumption infected the lot."

"Take my hand and I will lead you into a gentler world, the world of true forgetfulness. You won't even know you're there. No pain, no confusion, an end to worry...relief."

"No thank you."

"You've grown too comfortable dreaming. I've stood back, not interfering...out of kindness, if you must know. Perhaps I took pity on you watching you struggle against consumption for so many years. Heroic, I admit. But my kindness has reached its limits. Your dreams of Gail are—how shall I put it?—unhealthy? For your own good, you must divest yourself of them. You must move on."

Freezing drafts raced about my room. Chilled, I shiver, "I want to see Gail again."

"No. Gail's a distraction. You need to lose some sleep. The time will come when you will no longer be able to tell the difference between day and night, when that thin membrane separating the conscious present and the dream tears, then you'll see me for the friend I am."

Frightened, I blurted out, "That's no cure."

'It's dementia, a kind of cure. Your mother can vouch for it. I'm sorry it's come to this. You leave me no choice. Keep more of Jennie's rags on hand. When the cure begins to work, you'll drool, strings of mucus running down your chin, lacing your white pillows pink. Waking moments you'll believe a nightmare. Bewildered, eyes dull, you'll look about and tonelessly ask an empty room "Where am I? Is anyone here? Who are you?" You'll hear no answers. Finally the day will come when you'll stop asking others questions and start asking yourself the only real question, "Does any of this matter?" By then you'll have forgotten Gail.'

"I'll never forget Gail."

The soft sulfur light of the waxing gibbous moon kept me awake; and I coughed and spit all night. By morning Jeanie's bleached rags, now bloodied, mount up beside my bed. I vaguely remember someone removing them. Only the thought of the big brown trout feeding in Knight's Pool comforted me.

People come and go passing in front of my window briefly darkening my room. I hear Roy's voice and Jeanie's in reply, garbled of any meaning. Once waking, stupefied, I saw a stack of mail on my tying table. At least two days' worth. I am too weak to reach for it.

Again dim light. Perhaps the sun in overcast. Perhaps the moon. I make out the red rooster stalking about my room. Awake yet exhausted, Gail's two pictures lay before me on the bread board. My eyes close awaiting her fingers to come alive and stroke my temples. Her dress rustles as she bends over me, and one of her hands rests light on my forehead as when my mother felt for fever. I reach up to catch her wrist and pull her down for a kiss. My hand closes on Jeanie's wrist. When her face appears I recoil with a groan. I am alone but for my roaming noble friend which raises its head and looks at me questioningly. I pat the bed, and it hops up flapping its wings.

Finally I fall into the terrified sleep of clenched jaw and grinding teeth. A railroad switching yard at night, the screech and banging of a train forming, swinging lanterns, pinpricks of light among the cars and flashes of lightening reveal low lying black storm clouds threatening a soaking. All about, the rumble of box cars, the slam and catch of couplings as the long train knits together. Tacked up placards flutter, proclaiming amid flashes of lightening that it is my carnival train, the train carrying my midway, my life to its next stop. Drenched, I wake up in a sweat, desperate to know the name of that stop.

This turmoil went on for three days. Then the fever broke.

## 23

## Opening Day

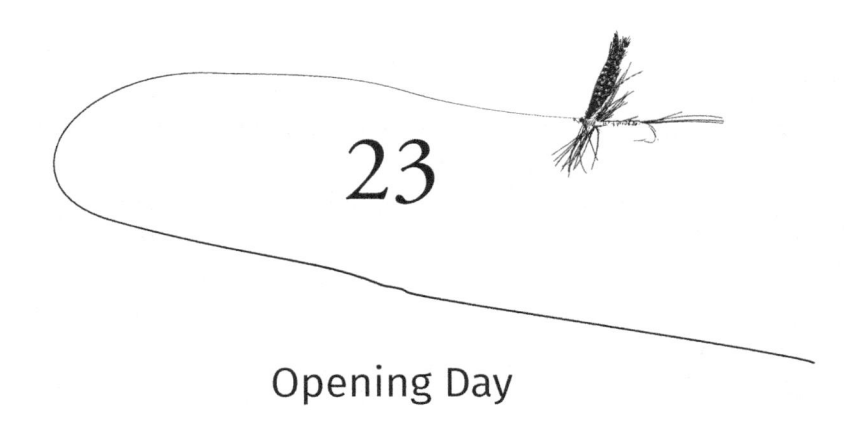

My noble red rooster crowed first light. Shaken, I open my eyes. It stood on my chest, looking down on me, blood on its beak, agitated. I stroked its head, my right hand bleeding. "Sorry; I forgot your dinner." Picking up the pouch of corn, I tossed out a blood-speckled handful on the floor. The rooster bowed and, flexed its legs, gliding off the bed. Thwack. Thwack. I drifted off mentally, scratching out an article on hooks. Visions of large stainless steel hooks and ocean fishing for ray off Florida pulled me deeper under the comforter.

That day, and for a week thereafter, a south wind blew a thaw through the Catskills. Daytime temperatures rose into the forties. The roads turned muddy, and the snow retreated, forting up under pine trees. By the end of the week, the Neversink had driven all remnants of ice downstream and was running full, bank to bank, black with melt water.

Cold, high water for Opening Day. Doubtless, the fish hunkered down bottom feeding. I went through my fly boxes. I will need sunk flies, flies designed to tick along a river's bottom. I have three Opening Day favorites. Two of the three I have already listed among my favorite flies. These are the Larva and the Bumblepuppy. The third fly I call the Little Wet. A simple dressing, muskrat-dubbed body and gray grouse hackle, I fish it in small sizes. Silver or gold wire can be wound around the body if the angler is so inclined.

Tying flies leaves me weak. Exhausted, sitting quietly by my window staring at the river, my eyes scan the dark water rushing through Knight's Pool. And I wonder whether Opening Day will see me catching the big brown trout living there. It is big enough to be reported in taverns and hotel dining rooms with envy, "Gordon caught a four-pound brown today." The word passes from bartender to waiter, and the following day, anglers notice me as I walk to the river. They murmur to each other, "There goes Gordon. Caught a huge brown yesterday." Surreptitiously, they spy on me. Inquiries are made. By the time word is carried back to Manhattan, the fish gains a few more pounds and the name of the fly lies wrapped deeper in mystery. They will need to write me and order it. Perhaps the fish might be worth an article.

Friday, the day before Opening Day, Jeanie kneads sweet dough in the kitchen. I hear the it slap down and the kitchen table jump. Bubbling yeast compressed two, three times to rise again, cinnamon rolls and coffee cakes for Easter. By an accident of the calendar this year, Easter comes the day after Opening Day. Jeanie is singing, "*Pardon each infirmity, open fault and secret sin.*" I have done enough penance for my secret sins.

Out my window, the circus that is Opening Day has come to the Neversink. Boarding house and tavern banners hawk, "Welcome Fishermen - Hot Buffet - Cold Beer." Wagons crowd the roads, shuttling anglers from Liberty's O & W station to Bradley or Claryville and every access point in between; some parties relive their boyhood, hiking to the river with full packs and tackle. White canvas tents rise in pastures and orchards. Campers stop at the Knights' back door to buy firewood. I hear the loud knocks and Jeanie's cheerful greeting, and from my window, I see them filling their arms with her split wood. Evening, fires blaze up; stew pots bubble; and beer bottles and hip flasks flash in the fire light. The orchard voices grow louder, and then laughter and song, the elation of men looking forward to a few days on the river and a bonus, a reprieve from dressing up for Easter services.

A few snowflakes fly past my window. More follow. Soon raking winds and great wet flakes cake the orchard's white tents and Bradley's white clapboard houses. In the cold, disconsolate campers stamp their feet and shake the snow from tent roofs and coats, more hip flasks, more shouts as tarps are stretched over firepits. By evening, huddled figures sit about sputtering fires, warming their hands. Veterans offer encouragement. "Just a freak storm. It'll be over in an hour. Blue skies tomorrow. You'll see."

The storm mounts, erasing roads, yards, and pastures. It chases Anson home from his chores. Jeanie was worried, and now relieved, the two are laughing as he stomps his boots on the back porch. The back door claps shut, a chair creaks, and two clunks follow one after the other as Anson slips off his boots. The stove door squeals open, and the aroma of Jeanie's bread fills the house. "One, two... yes, six loaves." A knife rasps. "Here's a heel, Anson." The thud of a Mason jar follows. "And apple butter." I hear a muffled thank you, a kiss, and a giggle. "Now for the coffee cakes and rolls, and we'll be ready for Easter." Baking pans scrape the stove's shelves, and the door squeals shut.

For no reason, I grow hopeful. I lay out my fishing equipment, admire my fly rod that Mills revarnished, grease my silk fly line with Mucillin, and squirt a few drops of oil into the gears of my reel. The afternoon I spend knotting together seven-foot leaders stout enough to turn over the Larva and Bumblepuppy. Checking the knots again, I coil them in my leader box to soak. Wet flies are clipped by pattern in fly boxes. Most likely no need for dry flies, but just in case risers show in the backwaters, I slide a small box of Quill Gordons in a jacket pocket. Wool pants, a tweed jacket, a sweater, and waders lay out on my chair.

Late afternoon shadows crowd the corners of my room. I tell them, "I'm warning you. I'll not be listening to your mournful notes tonight."

The shadows laugh. "And how do you propose to stop us?"

"Letters...*Where the Barefoot Boys Fish*...and Gail's picture."

A cackle from one dark corner startles me. My noble friend. I balance bread board, letter paper, and pen on my knees. The scratching begins. I write Dr. Griffin and Guy Jenkins for a report on the flies shipped them, and I inquire if they need more, then a short letter to Skues.

Letter writing done, I pick up the back copies of *Forest and Stream* with the *Barefoot Boys* serial. Shadows creep from the corners and crowd my bed, silent specters waiting for me to pause in my reading. Imagining myself the barefoot boy I once was in Carlyle, I savor each scene. "It looks like I've found the antidote to unwelcome guests," I say out loud to the milling shadows.

Coughing, gagging, I spit into a bleached white rag. Lying back, I wipe my mouth, fold it over, pat my lips, and throw it on the newspapers lying beside my bed. Staring at the ceiling, flushed, I wait until the waves of nausea pass and then drink a finger of bourbon to clear the taste from my mouth.

I think about my own barefoot boys: Christian, Roy, Anson, and Bruce. And I think of other barefoot Catskill boys, Stephen Crane and John Burroughs, and recall with pleasure their stories. "I must reread 'Speckled Trout,'" I tell myself.

With the storm upon us, no moon tonight. Neyle and Josephine come to mind, and so too, Neyle's flute, and I think of wood thrush returning to sing in the uplands. Calling to mind other cold Opening Days, I rest preoccupied with riverbanks and currents, roll casts and high water, chill fingers and doubts. Spring's high, dark waters sap a fly fisher's confidence. Early season success goes usually to bait fishermen. Signs advertising worms tempt even the most committed purist.

The sight of my fishing jacket transports me to the dusty road in front of Herron's. I see myself standing alone, looking up into a burning sun and smelling the dry dust kicked up by a hurrying carriage. Yearning, aching for her, for Gail, I throw back my covers and grope out of bed like one blind. It is time I wore her colors. Bundling ribbons together, I pin to my jacket her colors, bright green and sooty gray, the color of her damsel flies. The colors darken under my tears as I fumble with the pin. The stained ribbons remind me of all that could have been. Alone, forever alone.

Throughout the night, a fierce north wind punished the Catskills. In the dark, it prowled about Knight's yard, growling, waking me and drifting snow to the sills of the downstairs' windows. It buried tents and firepits, and at first light, frostbit and hungry, struggling campers dug down like squirrels to recover tents, pots, packs, rods, and tackle. In the morning, I hear the scrape of highway plows and the blowing of straining oxen. Anson shoveled a path from the orchard encampment to the road. Without ever casting a line, subdued anglers began their miserable trudge back to Liberty and the railroad, but not before Jeanie called them in for sweet rolls and hot coffee. Her compensation—the only compensation she expected—smiles and thank yous. As each left, I heard her "Happy Easter," and I think maybe it is time to make peace with her. Maybe. The idea still angers me.

Opening Day proved to be just another day in my room. If the cold breaks in a day or so with seasonable temperatures following, the river might be fishable by week's end. The old trout in Knight's Pool will rest safe until then. From the kitchen, I heard the back door open and Christian's "Hello." Jeanie shouted up, "Christian's here with your mail."

Christian dropped the mail on my bed. "Do you mind?" he said moving the jacket and clothes from my chair next to my tying table.

"No. Make yourself comfortable. You see the brandy and glasses on my tying table. Help yourself." I picked up the mail and riffled through about a dozen letters. One from New Jersey, not in Mother's hand.

"Didn't even string up my rod," Christian began. "Pulled a few campers out of drifts and gave them rides to town."

"Anyone out fishing?" I asked offhand as I opened the letter from South Orange.

"A few rode horses right into the river and fished from horse back. No locals out, a sleigh or two. Bait fishermen crowded the bridges fighting for a place on the railings. Didn't hear of anything but a few stockers being caught."

"That's the best news I've heard today." The bottle of brandy clinked against Christian's glass. Reading the letter from South Orange, I hardly heard Christian ask, "Should I pour one for you?" Mother will not be coming to Liberty. A disappointment, but what was more disappointing was the reason. My cousins reported she slept whole days, waking only for a little consommé from her nurse. Mother was dying. My cousins advised against visiting.

Christian caught my concern but went on, "The townspeople are digging out the churches for services tomorrow. You going?"

"Do I ever?"

"No. We could be fishing in a few days…"

"…if the weather cooperates." I was about to tell him the story of Habersham going north too early, but I caught myself, remembering I had told him that story the last time he visited. And then I started, "Skues…" and stopped myself again. Christian had heard all my Skues' stories more than twice. So I broke off and said, "Check that big box in the corner. There are some trolling spoons in it."

My stock of stories dwindles to a well-honed few. Stories of Savannah, Habersham, salmon flies, Skues, Halford, England's chalk streams, hook styles, fly tying materials, and so on. I repeat them over and over, and am beginning to hear from my visitors, "I must be going" or "I'll be late for an appointment…or work…or the family." Take your pick. I cannot blame my "barefoot boys."

And then there are the stories of my better days. A few years ago fishing Knight's Pool, I caught eleven good-sized trout in an hour and a half, the largest a sixteen-inch brown, and then there was that day, so many years ago, when at eighteen or nineteen, I caught forty trout in Bellefonte, the feat written up in the local newspaper; and the days in Wisconsin and Michigan where searching for healing springs, I found superb bass fishing. Then there were the days fishing for smallmouth bass on the Delaware, late September, after the frosts. The smell of wood smoke from our warming fires comes back, and with it, the sweet perfume of fallen moldering apples. Then there was the day bass fishing on the Delaware that I caught a thirty-inch brown trout, the largest trout I ever caught. It had to be returned because trout season was closed. But I am repeating myself.

And silently, I wonder about Mother's decline and whether she will recover. And it occurs to me I might never speak with her again. The words shatter something deep within me, and a chasm opens at my feet. I grow slack, sway as if to topple, then catch myself. And think, "It is the way of things." Words I have said so often to myself when consumption drained me. I look over at Christian bent over my box of miscellany. He fingers the gadgets and lures, and his eyes shine with their possibilities. No purpose served in sharing my upset.

Christian sorts through the box, holding up a bait casting reel admiringly, "Nice."

"Take it."

"Are you sure?"

"Yes, the spoons are on the bottom."

"The ones with the red bead eyes."

"Take two. That should hold you for a while."

"Thank you. I best be getting home. My wife will need me. More shoveling. It's still coming down. Anything else I can do for you."

"Go. I need to dress for dinner, and then I'll read some."

Christian looks up thoughtfully. "Mr. Gordon, we could take my wagon and fish from it in the big pool below York's."

I laugh. "Go home and shovel.... We've got all spring."

The rest of my correspondence I read sitting by my window overlooking the river. More fly orders. The river is clearing. I can see bottom along the edges and not an angler in sight. A few dark mayflies pop to the surface, float a dozen feet or so drying their wings, and then flap ascending from the river. A splash and then another. Bubbles as large as one of Jeanie's serving bowls upended. It is the big brown trout. I see its shadow in the roiled water and watch its rhythmic rises until nightfall. With Mother dying, I must, more than ever, touch the brown's smooth cold skin to renew my hold on this world.

# 24

## My Nephew's Visit

Opening Day come and gone, a surprise visit proved Jeanie had broken our truce. A knocking at the back door carried up through the heat register. Too early for Roy or Bruce. Christian's voice mumbled to Jeanie. "Mr. Gordon's nephews, the Spencer brothers from South Orange."

"Thank you for coming," Jeanie said. Then her voice dropped, and I caught only the words "short of breath" and "failing." She shouts up, "Mr. Gordon, you have visitors." More whispering, and then I hear them on the stairs.

"Brought you a surprise, Mr. Gordon," Christian announced. "One says he's your namesake."

My nephews followed him through the door. Dark suits, high collars, and black ties, as though attending a board meeting, both more somber than I remember. Nonplussed, I blurted, "Why did you come up here?"

"To see our favorite uncle?" Gordon, the older of the two, putting it more as a question than a statement of fact.

I just looked blankly at them. "A letter would do."

They laughed. "We wanted to see how you're doing." Silence and then one offered, "Maybe get one of your stories."

I fell silent again, expectant, wondering if this was their roundabout way of getting down to business, the business of telling me the news of Mother's death. I wrestled with this fact quietly.

"You both look healthy," I said and then looked away dreading their report. Then remembering my manners, I rallied, "Find a seat."

They both looked about. Gordon took the chair at my tying table, careful not to step in the red splotches on Jeanie's news sheets. Gently nudging aside my red rooster, Edward, the younger brother, opted for the windowsill, the warmest seat in the room.

To break the silence, Edward said cheerfully, "It's good to see you again, Uncle Theodore. The last time we saw you was three years ago when we fished the Esopus together."

"Did you bring your equipment?"

"No. Came up on a lark. Taking the train back this afternoon. If Father gives us time off, we'll be back in June to fish."

"June is always good," I said turning to Christian, "Christian knows the river. He could take you out. I've been too blowed to fish."

"We could all go to Claryville for a day," said Christian.

"I'd probably spend the day stretched out in the back of your wagon."

None of us believed they would return in June. "How's the family?

"Father's driving us hard. But you know him," Gordon offered.

Hesitant at first, I finally asked, "What's the news on Mother?"

"Nothing's changed since I wrote you. She sleeps mostly. Aunt Emma looks in on her every few hours, and we have a local lady taking care of her needs."

"No pain?" I asked expectantly.

"No pain," Gordon said. "She's more and more befuddled as the days go on. She hardly knows when anyone's in the room. Aunt Emma thinks she's close to the end. She does not even recognize Aunt Emma anymore."

"That's difficult to believe. Aunt Emma was one of her favorites... as was your mother, of course."

"I see you have a faithful companion," Edward said, eyeing my red rooster.

"Yes. The perfect guest. He's not a snoop." I made a face and pointed downstairs toward the kitchen. Christian laughed.

"Your companion's balding."

"It goes toward his board and room."

Both my nephews grinned.

"Want a touch of something to take the chill off?"

Both refused. "Too early in the day. Wouldn't want Father to smell it on our breaths."

The conversation drifted to the weather when I broke in, "Is there any hope Mother will recover her senses?"

"No. When she's awake, we read your letters to her, and she says they're very nice. But she becomes confused when we tell her they're from you. She doesn't recognize your name anymore."

"I travel down and see her before she goes."

"Only if your health permits. No one will hold it against you if you don't make the trip. It won't make a wit of difference to her."

"No matter what that busybody downstairs says, I'm doing just fine. A day or two out fishing with Christian and my breath will return. It's the same every spring. Oh, by the way, thank you for the pressure socks. They're just the ticket." Pulling up a pants leg, I ran my hand up and down the elastic sock to show I was wearing them.

"Happy to help."

"Anything else?"

"No."

"Have you two done any fishing?"

"Not since the Esopus. We had a great time with the rainbows, didn't we?"

I nodded. "That was three years ago?"

They looked at each other and then Edward said somberly, "Just want you to know that we miss you, Uncle Theodore. We miss your stories."

"Bring your equipment next time. We'll fish together. That's better than a story."

"One story from the old days. Please," Gordon pleaded.

"Let me think. I don't want to retell a story you've already heard a half-dozen times before." I looked over at Christian and winked. Christian chuckled.

"Did I tell you the one where I was written up in a local newspaper? It's from the old days. Must be thirty years ago."

"No," they both said.

"I was staying at a snug hotel in Bellefonte a small Pennsylvania town.... You been to the country near Carlisle? You have relatives there."

"Once," Gordon said. "It was for Uncle Mason's funeral."

"Fishing?" The brothers shook their heads.

"Too bad. It's great trout country. Anyway, a river ran through the town, and every evening the surface of the river was covered with rises, some from pretty good-sized speckled trout. Christian, could you pour a little brandy for me? This talking's making me dry." Christian handed me a jelly glass half full of brandy. The brothers looked at each other without remark. Their father was always pointing out the evils of drink, and I was his number one exhibit proving its ill effects.

A sip and I winked at them. The brothers smiled weakly. "In those days, I was a wet fly fisherman. Most of the active insects in the river there were small, nothing like what we have up here. The trout sipped them non-stop for hours. I had few small flies and no small hooks. The flies the trout were taking were light dun about a quarter-inch long. The local fly shop did not have small enough hooks, nor a fly to match it. I know because I bought what the clerk recommended, and it was wrong on the color."

My throat tickled so I took another sip of brandy. "I stripped one of my small flies. A little gray wool raveled from a sweater and some dun hackle unwound from another of my flies did the trick. The next evening, I started in casting my jumble of a fly. The fish were jumping as usual. This river was slow moving and shallow with watercress and forget-me-nots along its edges. After some experimentation, I fished it dead drift just under the surface and started catching fish immediately."

My throat tickled again. Afraid of gagging, I downed a large swallow of the brandy. The tickle went away. The brothers looked at each other disapprovingly.

"The hotel owner promised me a trout dinner if I caught a few for him. I took a large creel. The more fish I caught, the more anglers appeared and collected about me casting. Most fly fished. I won't say they beat the river to a froth, but they came close. So I moved downstream from the town. More jumping trout and with the same fly, fish after fish went into my creel. No one else caught a fish. I stopped at forty.

"One of the fly fishers sidled up to me as I climbed out of the river. He was the editor of the town newspaper."

"'That was some exhibition you put on, sir,' he began."

"'It was a rare day even for me,' I replied."

"'What did you catch them on?'"

"I showed him my miserable tie.

"He looked perplexed but then asked, 'May I have it? I want to do an article on you.'

"'Yes, you can have it, but only if you put my name in the headline.'

"'Of course,' he replied.

"The article appeared next day, and Theodore Gordon became a celebrity for ten miles around. The forty trout went to the hotel owner who promised me two more free days of lodging. I stayed and had a few more days of superb speckled trout fishing. The fish were large. Probably the best speckled trout fishing I've ever had, even the times I fished Maine.

"Anything else?" I asked.

"No."

"Well, that's good because you've tired me out." The burden of sociability drained me, and I began a racking cough. By the time the cough ended, and I could spit and wipe my mouth, my good cheer and the good cheer of all had died. Edward had covered his mouth and nose with a handkerchief. Looking about, I whispered, "Christian, I need my sleep. Why don't you take these gentlemen back to the station?"

"Sure, Mr. Gordon." He gestured for the brothers to hurry along.

"I appreciate you coming. Give my best to your father. He's always provided safe haven for Mother and me." Not wanting to appear too curt, I added, "Let's try to get together in June when I'm stronger." They murmured their "next Junes" without conviction. "And on the way out, tell the fat lady downstairs to mind her own business."

They did not pass along my message. And knowing their father, I knew they would not be back in June.

# 25

## Death

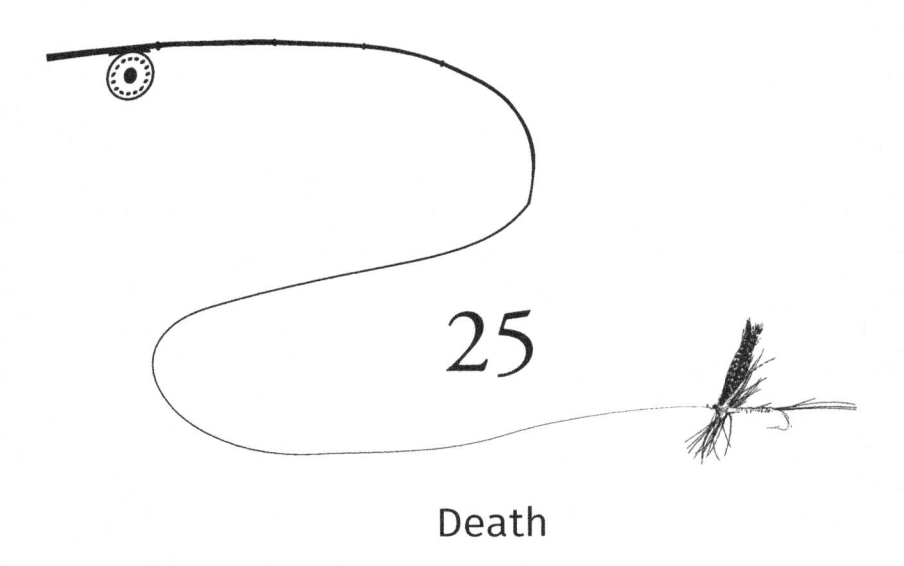

The big brown trout foraged Knight's Pool all afternoon. The pool formed years ago when the bridge to Liberty was thrown over the Neversink. The bridge abutments pinched the river, slowing it, and spinning out eddies along the river's rush. The big brown trout took up residence in an eddy just upstream of the bridge, and it was there it waited for hapless insects caught in the river's tow.

All day, traffic crowded the bridge. Wagons rumbled over it, making deliveries. Children trudged over it, laughing and teasing on their way to and from school. Housewives hurried over it, running errands. Men in dungarees, bib overalls, and collared shirts crossed and recrossed it, going to and from nearby farm fields or their jobs in Liberty. Everyone stepped lively. It had been unseasonably warm the last several days, and the snow dropped Opening Day had all but disappeared. The river ran clear.

The rumbling wagons and trembling bridge abutments did not bother the big brown trout. It fed leisurely on Iron Duns, gray mayflies, which dribbled from the rapids at the head of the pool. Responding to the urge to reproduce, the duns left their underwater homes and swam to the surface where they floated helplessly for several yards. Patiently, they marked time, waiting for their two large smoky gray wings to dry. Also marking time, the big brown trout awaited the duns' approach. Before they could fly off, the big trout sucked them down. On nearby boulders, black birds and robins roosted, marking time as well, waiting for the duns that did escape the river to fly upward. Once airborne, the birds fell on them. The duns, slow, clumsy fliers, had no defense against maw and beak, except their courage and their great numbers. While the trout and the birds feasted, fully occupied, many duns escaped. On them hung the future of the species.

At a break in the parade of duns into the pool, the great trout looked up at the white clapboard house beside the pool and at the thin man sitting by the second floor window. It saw a brief flare of light and the thin man staring down at it. It noted the man's interest and noted also the man too was marking time. The great trout had seen such patient interest before. This man was dangerous.

Watching the trout from my second floor window, I noted the trout's interest in me, then sighed, rolled, lighted a cigarette, and smoked in slow puffs. The big brown porpoised as it fed. It was of the yellow variety. I calculated the distance between its dorsal fin and tail at fifteen inches. Surely, a four-pound fish.

Many knew of the trout. The neighbor lady across the road noticed it when she tended her kitchen garden. She told her husband about it, and the husband offered the big trout minnows hooked through the lips. The trout ignored them. School boys spied it one day when crossing the bridge, and ever after, they stopped and leaned over the railings for a glimpse. The school boys offered it fat night crawlers. The trout ignored them. The great trout's reputation spread to Liberty, and fly fishers from Liberty standing in the rapids above Knight's Pool offered the full inventory of their fly wallets. The great trout ignored them all. And so its reputation spread to Manhattan and beyond. Some locals, drunk, waded the pool with pitchforks. The trout eluded them, inserting itself in a crevice between the bridge abutments. Any angler that caught this trout would be famous and justly so.

Weak from night sweats, I sat watching the trout go about its business. Late morning, Jeanie Knight brought a pot of tea and a bowl of oatmeal swimming in fresh cream. She scolded me for being out of bed.

Pointing down to the pool, I told her stonily, "I am watching my best nurse."

She leaned over me. "Where?"

"The big trout just above the bridge."

Jeanie looked down again. "A fish?"

"My adversary in the lists."

A blank look, then with disgust, "Your best nurse just brought you breakfast!" With that, she stomped down the stairs to her kitchen.

The oatmeal restored me and my breath returned. And with the return of my breath came a plan. That evening, I would try for the trout.

By now, the emergence of Iron Duns had ended for the day. In the frenzy following emergence, spurred on by hunger and thirst and the deeper realization that their hours were numbered, the duns escaped to nearby trees and bushes where they took a day to molt. Their wings lost color and their legs and bodies desiccated, hardened, and darkened. Now mature spinners, they looked forward to the evening when they would swarm above the rapids, dance, mate, and die.

Looking through my fly boxes was the first order of business. I combed each, inspecting every wing, hackle, tail, and fly body until I found three-eyed flies and one snelled fly that would match the Iron Dun spinner.

Throughout its day, the Neversink wears every color light can cast. And the river plays with these colors, endlessly bouncing them on and off every insect drifting in or on its currents. A fly fisher cannot step into the same river twice. So also a fly fisher cannot cast the same fly onto the same river twice. A fly will change color a dozen times as it floats, tilting to and fro, in or on the current. It can be as bright as the white reflection of a kingfisher's wing when it wheels to dive. It can take on the many greens of the aspen, alder, and pine hugging the river's banks. And it can be as dull as the grays and tans of overhanging slate, sandstone, and limestone ledges. Add to these colors the shifting colors of the evening sky. First comes the silver light, then the burnished bronze sliding into gold. A pulsing pink follows and then an intense, blinding orange. The orange will linger, rolling out at its feet a fragile violet which bathes all insects, trees, ledges, anglers, and turns the very air violet the instant the orange quits.

With their hyaline wings, Iron Duns become garish at sunset. The evening light reflects off their glassy, crusted bodies, and their wings radiate like a prism backlit. My flies for evening fishing have hard translucent hackles and glossy bodies, either peacock quill or natural fur dubbing ribbed with gold and silver wire and tinsel. The hard, translucent hackle reflects the many colors and half colors bouncing off the river's surface. In short, the hackle becomes the color of water. Thus, I am partial to a glossy fly, preferably gray, a neutral color that easily accepts the colors the river casts, a fly receiving the light and reflected light the same way a natural insect receives and casts off light.

Evening was some hours off. Catching the large brown would make up for a winter of disappointments. It had been hard not only on me but on Mother also. My feet and lower legs swell if I sit or stand for too long. My doctors at Loomis diagnosed a weakening heart and prescribed pressure socks. At their urging, whenever I can, I write or tie flies in bed, my legs elevated on a pillow.

Now to finish my plans for taking the big brown. A small bell sits on my bedside table, a gift from Jeanie. I rang it, and Jeanie appeared filling the doorway.

"Yes, Mr. Gordon."

"If you would be so kind, I would like a simple sandwich in my room instead of coming down for dinner."

"Of course, Mr. Gordon. What would you like?"

"Some of your ham, thinly sliced, with Anson's special mustard. Oh, and a glass of milk." Like some wayward child planning to skip school, I decided to creep out of the house while Jeanie and Anson were eating dinner with the other lodgers.

The ham sandwich arrived, waking me up from a nap. Jeanie approved that my legs were draped over a pillow. She smiled. "When you're finished, just ring the bell, Mr. Gordon." She placed the tray on my lap. "I'll be downstairs in the dining room." She left quickly.

Carefully, I sat up and swung my legs off the bed. Placing the tray on my bedside table, I slipped into my waders, arctics, and tweed coat. Patting the coat pockets, double-checking, the flies were there as was my leader box and a seven-and-a-half-foot soaked leader. Pulling the three sections of my rod out of its case, I affixed the reel. Ready to go. Tiptoeing to the door, I gently opened and just as gently closed it. The stairs squeak under Jeanie's and Anson's weight but not mine. Confidently, I placed my full weight on every tread. Silence. The tiptoe across the kitchen was just as silent.

The backdoor opened with a faint, high-pitched squeak. I heard Anson say, "Someone's at the back door."

Jeanie replied, "You enjoy your dinner. I'll check." Jeanie's chair scraped on the dining room wood floor.

Closing the backdoor brought another slight squeak. I ran down the back steps, made the yard, and hid behind the woodpile. The back door opened. And just as hastily closed. "No one here, Anson," Jeanie called back. I heard her heavy steps crossing back through the kitchen, waited for a few minutes, and then walked quickly to the river.

Sliding down the bank, I assembled, and strung my rod. Creeping along on hands and knees, I pulled up a short cast from the great trout's hold. Above the rapids, spinners mated, dipped their abdomen in the surface of the river, ejecting their eggs; then, their destiny fulfilled, they dropped inert onto the breast of the Neversink. The great trout sucked them in, unhurried. Elsewhere in the pool, above and below the great trout, other trout, smaller trout, fed noisily.

A dark, sparse version of my Quill with splayed wings was my first choice. My leader tapered to a 1x tippet, as light as I dared go. If the trout ran under the bridge, I needed to turn it. Even then, the 1x would be barely sufficient.

My plan was to cast a few feet above the great trout, shake out slack, and let the fly dead drift over it. The problem with casting downstream to a feeding trout comes when it does not rise to the fly. The angler must then retrieve it without raising the trout's suspicions. This trout did not grow to its great size ignoring such oddities as a fly floating downstream dead drift and then turning around to swim upstream. Not to raise its suspicions, my plan was to roll cast the rejected fly across the river away from the trout and then to retrieve it quickly, skipping it back. No better alternative presented itself.

Gauging its feeding rhythm, I made the cast. The fly alighted softly just above the great trout. Slack was shaken out, and the fly bobbled when it came to the outermost current of the trout's eddy. The current caught it as I had hoped and shunted it into the trout's feeding lane. The trout did rise, but it picked off a natural spinner floating next to my Quill. The roll cast and a mend snapped the fly and the fly line away from the trout. As the fly landed, a small trout went for it, but I skipped the fly back before the small trout could grab it.

My legs were beginning to pain. And I craved a cigarette. Except for its wings, the fly looked right on the water next to the naturals, catching and reflecting the setting sun as it threw a deep violet over all. In a few minutes, it would be dark. One more cast. Staying with my Quill, I flipped it onto the same spot my first cast hit, shook out slack, and watched the fly. This time, no naturals floated nearby. As the Quill again slid around the outside ring of the eddy, I saw the river's surface lift as the broad back of the trout displaced several square feet of water. But no rise. It found my fly wanting and sank slowly back to its hold. Disappointed, I slapped the roll cast and the fly flew across the river. To myself I said out loud, "There's always tomorrow." My fly began to drag when a small trout took it. As a matter of reflex, I set the hook and then, disgusted, began pulling the small trout in. A few feet into the retrieve, a wake shot across the river and took the small trout down. It was the big brown. I reared back and pulled up the large trout with the small trout clamped across its jaws. One of the large trout's eyes fixed me. And then it shook its head as if in anger, dove, and snapped my leader.

Too dark for another cast. Slowly climbing back up the bank, drained, I pulled apart my rod and crept up the back steps, opened and closed the back door slowly, noiselessly, then tiptoed across the kitchen and made the stairs to my room. The low murmur from the dining room reassured me Anson and Jeanie had not heard.

Coat, arctics, and waders I stowed on my chair. Pulling my nightgown over my head, I crawled into bed. The milk and ham sandwich sat untouched. I gulped the milk and eagerly nibbled the edges of the sandwich. My noble cock slept on a windowsill undisturbed. Pulling out the corn pouch from under my pillow, I threw a handful in its direction. The clatter woke it, and it sailed off the sill. Thwack, thwack. With its claws clicking on the floor, it hunted for stray kernels. Now and again a thwack jolted me.

How can I ever tell Christian about the large brown? With a sly smile, he'd ask whether I was fly fishing or bait fishing. I am not prepared to argue the issue, so I thought better of telling him...or Roy. Roy wouldn't say anything to my face, but he'd come to the same question secretly that Christian would say aloud.

...minnows...

...it'd been years since I fished minnows.

The last time was in Wisconsin. Accompanying my mother on one of her trips to Michigan to take the waters, we decided to travel home separately. She returned to South Orange on her own while I booked passage on a lake steamer to Milwaukee and from there took a short train ride north to Oconomowoc. On its doorstep, I found a huge lake, a clean hotel, and a solicitous staff. It was a place of long days and long vistas with sweet air and soft breezes. And it was inexpensive. I trolled spinners baited with minnows. My young guide rowed for hours, skirting the edges of weed beds. He let me loll, attending to my every need. The boat rocked me to lethargy. The warm sun, the freshly scented air, the lightly rippling lake, and thin scudding clouds whispered serenity. Relaxed, I rested between tugging bass and pike. For once, my good luck held and my breath did not falter.

...the big brown...

...a more pressing matter...

Why did the big trout refuse my Quill? Was it the hackle, wing, body, or tail? One or more of the four was wrong. Possibly the wings. Its wood duck flank feathers did not show up as brilliant as the natural wings. I suspected that on the first cast. I should have changed flies then, but the dimming light made me impatient. Again. Tomorrow, I'll try a wingless version with stiff glossy hackles.

Throwing off my covers, I retrieved a box of Quills from my jacket. Back in bed, I did, as I have so often done, took one out and fondled it in my palm. My eyes traced the banding of the peacock quill, dark gray to light, and light to dark gray, and then the lemon-tinted tail whisks as well as the shaded duns and lemons of the wings. And I marveled at the sparse, stiff, glossy dun hackles wound for the legs.

My Quill is as ethereal as any mayfly. Breathing on the fly, it danced in my palm. On a breeze-kissed river, it will dance forever. Name the river, any river. It will dance there! It is so, so alive.

...tomorrow I'll tie my Quill without wings, only hackle. To ensure the hackles show up brilliantly in the evening light, the fly will be dressed with two hackles.

...but I am counting on the evening light being as it was this evening...foolishness. In the mountains, no one can count on the weather being the same from one day to the next, nor even from one hour to the next....

...the best plan is to tie a fly for a bright evening and another for an overcast dimly lighted evening....

...a sparse tie will show better in dim light...the hackle wings appearing indistinct.... Yes. The sparse tie gives just the hint of a wing. That is all the large trout sees of the naturals' wings on a dim evening.... Yes...just the suggestion of wings...translucent wings.

...also the sparse tie will lie in the film...just like the spent Iron Dun spinners.... To make sure of that, I'll snip off a few of the hackles barbs from beneath the fly.... That should do it....

...perhaps...

...categorical statements are beyond me...

...Halford's absolutes gave me the confidence to commit to dry fly fishing. But he had overstated his case and my absolute commitment was short lived....

My break with Halford was not on principle. I have a hard time admitting this even to myself. Halford helped me. He sent me forty-eight of his hand-tied flies, many his own dressings. I never sent him one of mine. And he recommended me to Marston. And because of my articles in the *Gazette*, I came to know Skues and became a name to anglers across the world.

But I was ungrateful. What I held against Halford is that he stopped answering my letters. He did not do so all at once. His replies grew shorter and shorter, and letter by letter, he left my life. In his defense, let me say I did whine about the lack of good fly tying materials here and the virtues of natural materials. I even explained my theory of mimicry. Mimicry ran against his theories. He made no comment. To illustrate, I followed up by sending him a grouse skin and part of a muskrat pelt. Again no comment. Nor did he acknowledge receipt of them. At first, I took his silence to mean I was on the wrong track. Later, I realized he did not consider me on his level. In one of his last letters, he asked, "What do you want from me?" I was tempted to reply, "Companionship," but did not. Finally, he stopped answering my letters altogether. No explanation, never even a short note making some excuse for cutting me out of his life. It angered me.

Who did he think he was? I had experiences to share. Significant experiences. He was not interested. My revenge was to lay the groundwork for a future where the New World of American fly fishing eclipsed the Old.... Enough said.

Then Halford died.

Upon his death, my feelings toward him didn't change. I'll never forgive his slight, so I dedicated to him, my first mentor, no more than a seven-sentence eulogy in an article devoted to colored leaders and the quality of evening light. In those seven sentences, I attributed to him my early case of dry fly fever and said little else. It was more about me than Halford. To stay in Marston's good graces, my eulogy was positive.

...but I went further and became a traitor to Halford....

A letter to Skues voiced my true feelings. Toward the end, Halford's writings rang with camp meeting rhetoric warning of the evils of wet fly and nymph fishing. He railed against Skues for popularizing upstream wet fly fishing. Unperturbed by the name calling, Skues continued to explain his views. His wet flies and now his nymphs have won wide acceptance. I should have forgiven Halford and overlooked his stridency as Skues did. When I told La Branche and Hewitt I would not be the fly fisher I am today were it not for Halford and his books, I was telling a half-truth.

When Halford cut me out of his life, I made sure to flush all certitude out of my mind. Ever since, I...deeply...deeply...resent confident generalization about trout fishing, and I avoid exchanging ideas with fly fishers who make them...unless they buy my flies.

Sometimes I explain my differences with Halford as being due to our natures. It was Halford's mission to ensure that each day fishing would prove his rules.... My mission is to revel in the wonder of each day.

...the big brown...

...perhaps it was the body of my Quill that alerted it to the fraud...

...yes...maybe the segmentation on the body did not show up as clearly as it does on the natural spinner...

...could try condor quill...

...but mine are ancient and too dark, too fragile...

...or adjutant quill. My adjutant is fresher. It will show the banding. I could use it on a sparse tie so in full light the segmentation shows up as it does in the natural spinners.

Perhaps...

I should try sparse ties with three different bodies, one each of peacock quill, condor quill, and adjutant quill. I'll varnish the hook shank before tying in the quill, so they'll be strong enough for the brown's teeth.

...or maybe I could go through my crewel for a dark gray to match the natural...a rib of silver wire would work well.... Gold would be better, but I am short it...my last came from some discarded gold epaulets.... Skues said he would look. I must remind him...

...so be it...silver...

I'll be tying and casting flies in which I lack full confidence...

...can't be helped...

...catching the large brown would be a great start to 1915...

...when tying up the flies for tomorrow, I'll keep wood duck sprigs for the tails....

...the Iron Dun has two tails so I will tie in only two wood duck sprigs...no more...it does not matter if it sinks...

...the large trout was taking spinners stuck in the film...

...the two sprigs should be sufficient to keep it barely floating....

I could twitch it to make it shudder like a spinner in its death throes.

The one advantage of fishing downstream is that the fly fisher can twitch a fly without arousing a trout's suspicions...

...but this trout is no ordinary trout so the twitching leader might put it off. Better to leave the fly float inert.... Yes, that is the safer course. An artificial can call attention to itself, but never to the point where it shouts desperation. That is so unlike nature.

The tail is right...

...perhaps....

If I catch the large trout, it will be a good day. My reputation will grow. Not just in Bradley but also in Liberty when the word reaches the hotels and taverns. And it will reach them. Christian, Roy, and Bruce will see to it. The news of the catch will probably be heard even at the Anglers Club in Manhattan.... Mr. Henderson will be pleased.... La Branche?...I cannot say.

I should have added a few more sentences in praise of Halford. Skues wrote a lengthy eulogy. He is more astute than I. Too late... Too late....

Perhaps the spinner with a gray wool body would fool the big brown. It would have to be a glossy wool, one with its oils...

...gray sheep...rare.... I must check my cardboard boxes tomorrow...dyed wool loses its oil and will sink...not the effect I seek....

The road calls me more of late. Probably consumption's old siren's cry. Now and again, I daydream of buying a truck and building a hut on its back. I should talk to Hewitt about my idea. The hut would have two cots and a tying table. There would be enough room to store my books, a typewriter, and all my fly tying materials.

Would that I could invite Norris to join me, our Walton, as good a companion as any angler could hope for. He died while I was traveling the South with Mother. Despite that unpleasant reality, I imagine us taking to the road together. Fishing the Catskills, I would guide him and return the favor of all I learned from his book. He never fished the Catskills' rivers for brown trout. They were introduced after his death. I see us wandering the Neversink and the valleys about, fishing the Beaverkill at Roscoe, the Willowemoc, the Delaware, and so many others. Meals in hotels or inns. Or over campfires when we travel beyond the last outposts of civilization. Norris would enjoy that. We could tie a small rowboat or canoe on the truck's roof and troll lakes for bass, pike, and muskellunge. We would travel to Carlisle so I could show Norris where I first cast the flies his book taught me to tie. And when winter came, we could drive south to Savannah and camp along the Vernon or another coastal river. We could visit Mary at Avon and eat seafood. And in the dead of winter with its vicious storms, we could travel farther south to Florida for bass fishing and shrimp with orange rice.

Along the way, we'd talk fishing. The Catskills, Maine, the Adirondacks, Halford, Skues, the dry fly, the nymph, the habits of brown trout, the merits of the rainbow trout, the destruction brought by logging and mills. And we'd plan trips to untouched waters—brook trout and grayling waters. We'd take turns tying fancy flies. Norris would tell me about Michigan's Manistee where he fished for grayling in the 1870s, and he would retell his story about fishing St. Mary's Rapids below Lake Superior. We would fish the Au Sable and freight our truck by railroad to Seattle and fish the Columbia River for salmon and steelhead.

This is my dream...if Jeanie's hymns hold any truth, maybe "in the sweet by and by" I will wash up "on that beautiful shore" and there find Norris extending his hand to help me to my feet....

Pleasant thoughts, but no help with the flies I must tie for tomorrow....

Where did I put the adjutant? The silver wire is on my tying table, as is the hackle, and the size #12 hooks.

Over my lifetime, I have corresponded with hundreds of anglers. Most I've never met. Yet reading their letters for the first time I never find them strangers. We fall into conversation as if picking up where we so recently left off. Was it yesterday? The week before? My Brothers and Sisters of the Angle. Every winter, I reread *The Compleat Angler* and go through Cotton's fly dressings for suggestions. And I have imagined more than once a morning walk up Tottenham Hill in the company of Father Izaak and Uncle Thad. Leaving London behind, it is a full day's walk to the Thatched House in Hodsden, another day's walk to Trout Hall, where I imagine Christian, Roy, Bruce, and my nephews will join us. Finally, we come into the land of trout where the streams flow silver and chatter in their riffles, the birds sing sweetly along the riverbanks, and cows graze in the meadows, noisily ripping fragrant spring green grasses. We catch several great trout, which feed us all, and we drink barley wine, tell stories, laugh, sing, and retire to beds and pillows smelling of lavender.

Such pleasures come rarely. There are the evenings with the Fly Fishers on the Little Beaverkill where we gather to celebrate Opening Day of trout season. Every morning, they walk unhurriedly to the river, their empty creels swinging. Evenings they turn their creels into the cook, wipe their rods down, carefully lay them flat on wall hooks or stand them upright in corners. Their silk fly lines they drape on chairs to dry them so in the morning they can grease them with deer fat.

Dinner is served in the mess hall where whiskey and brandy bottles are ubiquitous. So many of the Fly Fishers are good storytellers, among them my client Granville Harman who never disappoints. In his accounts, fish grew longer and fought harder than the rather ordinary trout resting in the mess kitchen sink waiting to be cleaned. Sometimes his audience demands he repeat a story from prior outings. Sometimes when Mr. Harman's stories stray into the outlandish, I glance at the other members for confirmation. For my benefit, they roll their eyes skyward. One time when I questioned the truth of one of his tales, Mr. Harman said, "A little fiction can make a real story more true." It took me a while to understand his words. But now I hear myself saying to Roy or Christian, "There is often more truth in fiction than non-fiction."

Tomorrow evening I will not have time to fish more than two

flies for the big brown. They must all be snelled. Otherwise, exchanging them will take too long and my legs will protest.

The truth is I, like most anglers, am no better than the rivers I fish. Fishing the Beaverkill the summer of 1906 made me a much better angler. The Beaverkill dominates this corner of the Catskills. It is a privilege to fish. To me it is a person, as most rivers to me are persons, a rather cold and standoff person, but a remarkable person nonetheless. The Neversink, my other great teacher, is a more light-hearted person than the Beaverkill. Its riffles and rapids flash and tumble cheerfully. The Beaverkill is never cheerful. It views all who enter it as adversaries. It is a stern proctor, objectively assessing an angler's skills. The Beaverkill allows for some good luck but not much. Because the Beaverkill does not encourage false confidence, anglers can trust that any trout they take from it is earned. It plays no favorites. It drives all who wade it to become better fly tiers and better fly fishers. This is a great gift.

...the kitchen stove damper squeaks, and Anson's heavy tread mounts the stairs. I must get some sleep. Tomorrow will be a big day....

Now that Opening Day has passed, we look ahead to May and June. In a few weeks, the Brown Drakes will appear. Anglers will be studying the surface of their river in anticipation. No rises yet. And it's then the angler remembers. Forget the rises. Forget the fish. Look up. A clump of Blue Flag bursts forth from a fern-covered bank. Robins, Purple Martins, and warblers twitter up and down the watercourse. The birds know the Drakes will come shortly. Was it the trumpeting of the Blue Flag that called the birds to this run at this hour? You reflect that if you knew what told the birds to gather, you would know your river. And you scramble to reduce it to words. But no words come. And you stand there, silent, aware of the current boiling about your waders; aware of the first golden Brown Drake fluttering upward; aware of a Robin plummeting to intercept it. No words. Just the river, the mayflies, the Blue Flag, and the birds. And you become a contemplative, pondering the heart of things.

I need my sleep....

My throat tickles...perhaps the figs will be in tomorrow's mail....

Coughing, I lean over the side of my bed to spit on the floor....

The blood drips down my chin....

Where are Jeanie's rags?

My noble friend cocks its head towards me...is it showing concern?

So unlike it....

## Author's Afterword

I promised to deliver Theodore Gordon's own story about himself. I have done so. Gordon's life displays two remarkable traits: objectivity and originality. These traits set him apart from all other prominent anglers of his age and gave rise to a new fly fishing experience. This new fly fishing experience, the American fly fishing experience, is his legacy to us.

Gordon's objectivity cannot be doubted. It began with himself. His greatest fear was becoming blind to his own shortcomings. So he devised the most rigorous of all tests for judging his own competence, namely, catching old brown trout out of public waters. In none of his writings did Gordon ever boast of a good day fishing private water. He refers to the Opening Day celebrations at the Brooklyn Fly Fishers' clubhouse on the Little Beaverkill where each spring he sold the members flies, yet he never mentions his own fishing experiences on their water where trout were planted and the property posted. According to local legend, Gordon did fish other Catskill club waters on occasion and was successful. None of these tales made their way into his repertoire of stories. Similarly, it should be noted what he considered his best day of fishing and his best year of fishing occurred on the public waters of the Beaverkill, Esopus, and the Neversink and involved large fish, mostly brown and rainbow.

Gordon's originality cannot be doubted. He applied his belief in the preeminence of a fly's color, a belief common at the time, to selecting his favorite flies. His list of flies is unique in fly fishing literature. Assembling lists of "killing" flies began with Dame Julia Berners' Treatise in the fifteenth century and has been a required chapter of every fly fishing book published since. What was original to Gordon's list is not the dressings of the flies. His contemporaries, both British and American, were familiar with these same patterns and dressings. What was original is his advice to carry these flies dressed in shades, commonly light, medium, and dark so that gaps in the color spectrum could be plugged.

Gordon's originality also shows up clearly in his invention of the sparse fly. The sparse fly could be fished both wet and dry, a novel concept in an age where dry fly and wet fly anglers drew battle lines and warred with each other. Gordon disclosed his unique approach to very few. It appears in his correspondence with Skues where he describes the sparse fly and how to tie it. It also appears in the words of Herman Christian and Roy Steenrod as recounted in Alfred Miller's face-to-face interviews with them. By keeping the sparse fly private, Gordon avoided controversy, thus giving his "rough and ready" fishing style room to develop apart from British influences.

Finally, Gordon's originality is on display in his strategy for finding the effective fly. The effective fly is the fly whose aspect on or in the water simulates the natural. This strategy he called "ringing the colors." Gordon coined this phrase and used it freely in his essays and letters. Pursuing this strategy, Gordon changed fly colors covering his spectrum and changed the position of the fly within the water column until he started catching fish. The strategy of "ringing the colors" is found nowhere in fishing literature before or since.

Two episodes recounted here require imaginative details. The first was the story of Gordon's romance with a young unidentified woman. Without doubt, Gordon fell in love. In his essays, Gordon relates spending long days in the company of a woman "chum" hiking and fishing. There are photographs of the two together and a photograph of her alone, which was found among his effects. Both Herman Christian and Roy Steenrod saw the two of them together frequently. They report that she was not a local woman and that the affair ended in disappointment for Gordon. He kept a photo of her close at hand throughout his last years. She could have been someone Gordon met in New York or Savannah. In the days before air conditioning, some Savannah residents traveled north to the Catskills for cooler summer temperatures. Before moving to New York, Gordon himself was one of them. More likely, it was a young woman he met at one of the Catskills' boarding houses. From his description, she was an athletic, physically fit, energetic young woman, informal in her manners, and unconstrained by Victorian mores. Gail was drawn to fit this profile.

The second episode requiring imaginative details was the story of Gordon's relationship with the Hendersons. They are stand-ins for the landowners along the Neversink who extended Gordon an open invitation to stay overnight with them. Often he obliged them with fish. Gordon was proud of his Neversink friendships. He must have been a good guest and a good conversationalist to win their regard for more than a single evening. In the Catskills, as elsewhere, homeowners follow the old adage that fish and house guests stink after several days.

In sum, this book exposes Gordon's person. He told and retold the stories recounted here. Taken together, they portray Theodore Gordon as he saw himself, namely, the skeptic, ever suspicious of fads, quick to dismiss ungrounded novel theories in favor of the proven practical. It was this attitude, his attitude, which molded modern American fly fishing.

# Bibliography

**Primary Sources**

McDonald, John, ed. *The Complete Fly Fisherman*. New York: Charles Scribner's Sons, 1947. An extensive collection of Gordon's letters and magazine articles.

Miller, Alfred W. *Fishless Days, Angling Nights*. Guilford, CT: The Lyons Press, 1971. Valuable for his interviews of Herman Christian and Roy Steenrod, Gordon's young fly fishing friends.

**Secondary Sources**

Askins, Justin, ed. *The Legendary Neversink*. New York: Skyhorse Publishing, 2007.

Conway, John. *Loomis*. Fleischmanns, New York: Purple Mountain Press, 2006.

Francis, Austin McK. *Land of Little Rivers*, New York: The Beaverkill Press, 1999. Contains photographs of Gordon artifacts and wonderful maps of the major Catskill rivers.

Peper, Eric and LaFontaine, Gary. *Fly Fishing the Beaverkill*, Helena, MT: Greycliff Publishing Company, 1998.

Schullery, Paul. *American Fly Fishing*. New York: The Lyons Press, 1987. Chapter on Gordon very helpful. A portion of an original manuscript from La Branche describing his relationship with Gordon in his later years alone is worth a read.

Solomon, Larry and Leiser, Eric. *The Caddis and the Angler.* Harrisburg, PA: Stackpole Books, 1977.

Van Put, Ed. *The Beaverkill*. Guilford, CT: The Lyons Press, 1996, 2002.

Wright, Leonard M. *Neversink*. New York: Atlantic Monthly Press, 1991.

John Gubbins fly fishes and writes in the Upper Peninsula of Michigan. He and his wife Carol live alongside the Middle Branch of the Escanaba River near the town of Ishpeming. Mr. Gubbins is author of *Profound River* and *Raven's Fire*, both critically well received novels. With the publication of *The American Fly Fishing Experience*, he has gone on to put the finishing touches on a fourth book about salmon fishing in Alaska. They have two sons, James, a mural artist who lives in Madison, Wisconsin and Alexander, a poet, who writes and teaches in the Upper Peninsula.

Made in the USA
Las Vegas, NV
19 October 2023

79382857R00125